INTERDISCIPLINARY APPROACHES TO CURRICULUM

Themes for Teaching

Thomas R. Post
University of Minnesota

Arthur K. Ellis
Seattle Pacific University

Alan H. Humphreys
University of Minnesota (Emeritus)

L. JoAnne Buggey
University of Minnesota

Merrill,
an imprint of Prentice Hall
Upper Saddle River, New Jersey   Columbus, Ohio

Library of Congress Cataloging-in-Publication Data

Interdisciplinary approaches to curriculum : themes for teaching /
   Thomas R. Post . . . [et al.].
       p. cm.
       Rev. ed. of: Interdisciplinary methods, a thematic approach / Alan
H. Humphreys. 1981.
       Includes bibliographical references and index.
       ISBN 0-13-227778-6
       1. Curriculum planning. 2. Interdisciplinary approach in
education. I. Post, Thomas Robert. II. Humphreys, Alan H.
Interdisciplinary methods, a thematic approach.
LB2806.15.I566   1997   96-19649
375'.001—dc20   CIP

Cover art: Superstock
Editor: Debra A. Stollenwerk
Production Editor: Patricia S. Kelly
Design Coordinator: Julia Zonneveld Van Hook
Text Designer: Linda M. Robertson
Cover Designer: Rod Harris
Production Manager: Pamela D. Bennett

This book was set in Times and Futura by Carlisle Communications Ltd. and was printed and bound by R.R. Donnelley & Sons Company. The cover was printed by Phoenix Color Corp.

 © 1997 by Prentice-Hall, Inc.
Simon & Schuster/A Viacom Company
Upper Saddle River, New Jersey 07458

Photo credits: p. 1, Barbara Schwartz, Merrill/Prentice Hall; p. 25, Anne Vega, Merrill/Prentice Hall; p. 43, Scott Cunningham, Merrill/Prentice Hall.

Printed in the United States of America

10 9 8 7 6 5 4 3 2 1

ISBN: 0-13-227778-6

Prentice-Hall International (UK) Limited, *London*
Prentice-Hall of Australia Pty. Limited, *Sydney*
Prentice-Hall of Canada, Inc., *Toronto*
Prentice-Hall Hispanoamericana, S. A., *Mexico*
Prentice-Hall of India Private Limited, *New Delhi*
Prentice-Hall of Japan, Inc., *Tokyo*
Simon & Schuster Asia Pte. Ltd., *Singapore*
Editora Prentice-Hall do Brasil, Ltda., *Rio de Janeiro*

PREFACE

The goal of education is not to increase the amount of knowledge, but to create possibilities for a child to invent and discover. When we teach too fast, we keep the child from inventing and discovering himself. Teaching means creating situations where structure can be discovered, it does not mean transmitting structure which may be assimilated at nothing other than a verbal level.

Jean Piaget

This book is about possibilities in teaching and learning. It is about the creation of effective learning situations for teachers and students. We have attempted to put together a number of themes that will allow you and your students to discover, explore, and experiment across the artificial boundaries of subject matter. In that respect, this book represents an attempt to integrate subjects. It is an attempt to create whole, rather than fragmented, patterns for learning. It offers you possibilities rather than finished products. It is *not* meant to replace your methods texts but rather to supplement those texts by using what has been taught to build an interdisciplinary focus using thematic units.

School subjects are typically taught as discrete entities. The teaching of math has nothing to do with the teaching of reading, which in turn has nothing to do with the teaching of science, and so on. There is little sense of "connectedness" among school subjects or among the parts of the day. It is taken for granted, apparently, that in time students will see for themselves how things fit together. Unfortunately, the reality of the situation is that they tend to learn what we teach. If we teach separation and discontinuity, that is what they learn. If we teach connectedness and integration, they learn that. To suppose otherwise would be wrong minded.

We propose in this book that you consider the idea of interdisciplinary teaching and learning beginning in the primary grades and continuing through middle school. We have identified a number of themes that lend themselves to integration. In each instance, we have selected topics for the themes that incorporate the humanities and communications arts, the natural sciences, mathematics, and social studies. We have even suggested linkages with music and art.

We do not propose that everything can or ought to be taught to students in an interdisciplinary fashion. There are some mathematics skills, for example, that you will continue to teach formally and discretely. This holds true for other subjects as well. The value of the thematic unit approach lies partly in its function as a focus on the application of the knowledge, skills, and values that are learned in the various formal subjects. Chapter Three contains themes to start you off in this interdisciplinary approach. You will find that the themes have differing emphases with respect to subject matter and academic disciplines.

This book is a sampler. The themes we selected vary in subject matter and will appeal to differing age ranges and learning styles. It should be understood, however, that a good theme can be pursued at any level of sophistication.

In the spirit of interdisciplinary instruction, we challenge you to begin to develop your own units once you feel comfortable with those that we have provided. No matter where you live or what you teach, you have the potential beginnings of an interdisciplinary unit. The rest is up to you and your students.

THE INTERDISCIPLINARY APPROACH

Interdisciplinary approaches to curriculum are not new. Almost one hundred years ago John Dewey and others of his era suggested that by applying ideas from one curriculum to another teachers would make the subjects more relevant and more interesting, and the student would be more likely to internalize important and deep connecting ideas. Dewey was an early advocate of promoting such deep understandings and identifying those themes that were the most significant from an intellectual point of view. He was also an advocate of developing a community of learners within the classroom and school who were able to discuss significant ideas comfortably and frequently.

Early discussion of interdisciplinary techniques embraced the "unit" concept, where curricula from various subject domains were focused around particular topics or themes. This book provides an updated view of these early ideas in a manner more appropriate for today's educational perspectives. Much has been done in research into how children learn, how students can be taught to function in cooperative settings, and how the evolving nature of curricular relevance can impact the school and its educational activities in a positive manner. This book is designed to be an extension of these earlier understandings and is meant to support and advance rather than to replace the basic methods courses in other disciplines.

As the various disciplines of mathematics, science, and social science redefine what is important from a curricular perspective in their various "standards" documents, schools are being asked to emphasize this, or to change that, in order to maintain and improve on the palate of educational offerings for their students. The only thing that each of the professional organizations agrees and actively supports is the concept of applying important concepts across disciplines and exploiting interdisciplinary connections when the opportunity presents itself. Further, these organizations (the national councils of mathematics, of science, and of the social studies) actively support the search for such interdisciplinary connections in the form of interdisciplinary approaches to curriculum.

This book is about techniques that classroom teachers can use along with their students to exploit such interdisciplinary connections. If we teach in a manner that isolates the various disciplines, then students learn that the disciplines are separate, unconnected, and discontinuous. If we teach them integrated approaches, that is what the students will learn. This latter perspective is much more likely to support the kind of intellectual understandings and knowledge structures necessary in the twenty-first century. This is not to say that specific knowledge within each of the major disciplines will no longer be important and therefore should no longer be considered as major outcomes of the educational experience—quite the contrary. At a time when the sheer amount of knowledge is estimated to double every ten to fifteen years, subject-specific understandings will be more important than ever. The nature of those understandings, however, will change dramatically. The nature of the disciplines will undergo significant change and at the same time the connections within and between these disciplines will become even more important. When we bring the power and knowledge base of a variety of subject areas to bear on a concept, a theme, or an idea, we are more able to deeply understand that concept, theme, or idea. It is equivalent to bringing an increased and improved arsenal of tools into the educational arena.

There is tremendous motivational appeal for students when interdisciplinary approaches are employed. This is partly because students play a very important role in the conceptualization, development, and implementation of these themes, and partly because they are so much involved in the process of helping these themes unfold. In short, interdisciplinary themes provide an excellent arena within which students can construct their own knowledge. We hope this book will help you and your students capture some of this excitement.

ORGANIZATION OF THIS TEXT

This book is divided into three chapters. In the first chapter, "Why? A Rationale for Interdisciplinary Teaching and Learaning," we discuss the rationale for interdisciplinary approaches, indicating that this approach is a natural consequence of modern cognitive psychology in general and nicely connects with the theoretical tenets of constructivism, a contemporary offshoot of cognitive psychology. We also address the position of multiple intelligences as espoused by Howard Gardner in his important book *The Frames of Mind* and discuss how this point of view supports the interdisciplinary perspective. The chapter also includes a discussion of appropriate evaluation techniques and a consideration of the pros and cons of interdisciplinary approaches.

Chapter Two, entitled "How? A Methodology of Thematics," is concerned with the pedagogical aspects of the identification and development of an appropriate theme, and then with the planning, implementation, and evaluation of student outcomes.

Chapter Three, by far the most voluminous of the three, is entitled "What? A Sampler of Thematic Units." In it we provide ten examples of themes used by us and by the teachers with whom we have worked. The topics are varied and represent all of the major subject areas, although because of our individual backgrounds they tend to emphasize mathematics, science, and the social sciences.

Finally, the book concludes with an epilogue and two appendices that contain many of the planning forms suggested earlier in the text, and a listing of some of the resources available to teachers interested in such approaches.

ACKNOWLEDGMENTS

We would like to thank the reviewers of this book for their helpful comments: Maureen Sherry Carr, *Western Oregon State College;* Barbara Kacer, *Western Kentucky University;* Cynthia G. Kruger, *University of Massachusetts, Dartmouth;* Donna J. Merkley, *Iowa State University;* and Steven H. White, *University of Kansas.*

CONTENTS

CHAPTER 1

Why?
A Rationale for Interdisciplinary Teaching and Learning

- Instructional Aspects of Interdisciplinary Methods
- Conditions Necessary for Interdisciplinary Teaching
- Pros and Cons of Interdisciplinary Methods
- In Summary
- Situating Interdisciplinary Studies within the Constructivist Framework
- Interdisciplinary Approaches and the Nature of Human Intelligence

In this book, we will attempt to help you build on what you have learned in your methods classes so that you can incorporate interdisciplinary methods in your classroom. We will help you choose instructional themes that will develop children's knowledge, skills, and values in a truly integrated way. Teachers and students tend to see learning in integrated "wholes." Unfortunately, however, textbooks devoted to single subjects and traditional assumptions about the division of learning into smaller parts called subjects make it difficult for teaching and learning to take place in such a way that large-scale problems are solved.

Too often we assume that all children need precisely the same skills and knowledge, and that we know the best way in which to teach them. This simply is not true. We do not know specifically where we want all children to end up, and we do not always know the best way for them to get where they are going. If we had such preconceived plans for children, all we would have to do is program their futures for them. This book is about possibilities, not predetermined ends. The activities included in this book celebrate differences in learning styles, interests, and abilities. They relate learning to conceptual structures that are built by teachers and students as they go about the process of solving problems.

We believe that interdisciplinary learning motivates students and teachers to want to learn. The best themes are those that you and your students think are important. We have found the themes included in this book to be stimulating, and we invite you to consider them, modify them, and build on them. There is no limit to the possibilities inherent in interdisciplinary learning. The value of cooperative learning invariably comes to the surface as children work together to solve problems that have a sense of reality about them. An attitude that learning is a process rather than a final product emerges. Interdisciplinary studies have meaning for teachers and students and often result in real change in the school and community. The experiences that children have as they work together using a variety of learning styles tend to stay with them. They provide the wonderful memories possible in the school experience.

The notion of an integrated approach to the curriculum springs from tenets of modern cognitive psychology and philosophy, which were developed by Jean Piaget, Hilda Taba, Jerome Bruner, Maria Montessori, and others. As indicated in Figure 1.1, these educators adopted a holistic view of the learning process and were concerned that children acquire an understanding of fundamental structures. Interdisciplinary units offer variations in the teaching and learning process that are usually not attainable with normal classroom procedures.

Interdisciplinary units also respond to the visions of educators in all curricular areas. They provide teachers with opportunities to respond to the standards identified by organizations such as the National Council of Teachers of Mathematics and the National Council for the Social Studies, as illustrated in Figure 1.2. By examining the organizational standards of these groups, you can see how best to meet the needs of your students. Selection of an appropriate theme is *not* left to chance but rather based on the needs and interests of learners. Standards help to focus the parts of the theme, thereby making the unit truly interdisciplinary.

INSTRUCTIONAL ASPECTS OF INTERDISCIPLINARY METHODS

There are six key instructional aspects of interdisciplinary methods that can positively impact children's learning. These are illustrated in Figure 1.3 and described in the following paragraphs.

FIGURE 1.1
What do leaders in the field have to say to support interdisciplinary methods?

Important learning and understanding require interaction and conversation.
L.S. Vygotsky

Promote the creation of an educational system that would nurture creative, inventive, and critical thought processes.
Jean Piaget

Learning the structure of knowledge facilitates comprehension, memory, and learning transfer.
Jerome Bruner

We need open and free access to the materials, systems, and agencies of learning.
Ivan Illich

The world is in the process of continuous and cumulative change.
Hilda Taba

An end result or desired behavior should be task analyzed.
Robert Gagné

It is important to become everything that one is capable of becoming.
Abraham Maslow

Discovery can be rote or meaningful, depending on the conditions under which learning occurs.
David Ausubel

Education should be based on children's spontaneous interest in learning.
Maria Montessori

The seven intelligences provide direction for unit development. A balance of learning styles must be considered.
Howard Gardner

The establishment of learning situations in which students are self-motivated would create the most effective environment for learning.
Zoltan Dienes

1. *Relevance*   By its very nature, a thematic unit contains relevant, timely, and important material. Although the teacher will normally identify the major topical area (i.e., energy, pollution, urban life, transportation, or calculation), it is the students who invariably personalize the particular approaches to be employed, the resources to be utilized, and the way in which reports will be conceptualized. Because students are so actively involved in the selection and shaping of the topical and subtopical areas, interdisciplinary approaches have a natural relevancy for students.

2. *Timeliness*   Interdisciplinary approaches permit in-depth consideration of topics, ideas, and events not normally considered in the school curriculum. This characteristic

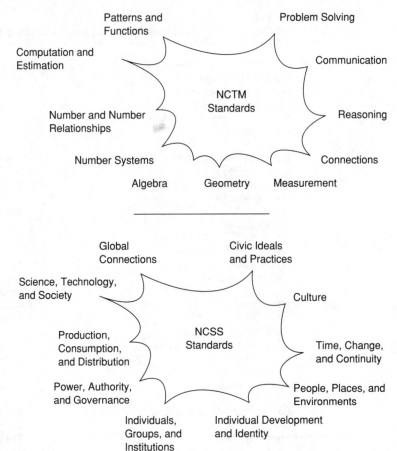

FIGURE 1.2
Possible themes selected from
NCTM and NCSS standards

promotes both teacher and student flexibility in the way in which the school curriculum is viewed and in the degree to which important ideas are accessible to scholarly inquiry. An interdisciplinary study can be launched at any time and need not be delayed until a related topic happens to appear in the textbook. Timeliness is related to the concept of relevance, the first key instructional aspect.

3. *Resource Accumulation (including technology)*   An interdisciplinary study at any grade level almost always begins with an open-ended problem. That is, we want to examine the way in which transportation has affected economic development in our town since 1950, or we are interested in the early development of precomputer calculational devices, or we want to contrast contemporary urban and rural life-styles. Because investigations of this type are not spelled out precisely and systematically by the text, they will invariably involve the use of a wide variety of resources. The text may be one such source, but it is never the only source. The school library, videotapes, local historical societies and museums, other students, parents, local businesses, CDs, computer programs, and the Internet all become fair game as resources and are accumulated for the investigation. Few would argue that the collection of information from such a broad spectrum is not an important skill as we move into the 21st century.

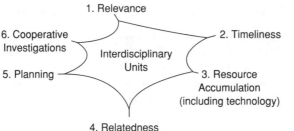

FIGURE 1.3
Instructional aspects of interdisciplinary units

4. *Relatedness* An interdisciplinary study will clearly demonstrate the interrelatedness of knowledge. Too often, knowledge is seen in schools as the accumulation of isolated bits of information that are to be memorized for an upcoming examination. An interdisciplinary study demands that information from a wide variety of sources be integrated into a unified, conceptual framework. Real-world knowledge rarely exists independent of context. Most occurrences in our daily lives are connected in one form or another to a wide variety of other occurrences, situations, and ideas. An interdisciplinary study therefore presents a true image of the nature of knowledge. One cannot help but develop a better appreciation of knowledge and learning in contexts that promote such interconnectedness.

5. *Planning* The initial open-ended nature of an interdisciplinary study requires much planning. Which topics and which subtopics are to be included in the investigation, what resources might be useful, which groups will pursue which subthemes, how student efforts will be partitioned, and how final reports will be conceptualized to convey maximum meaning and generate interest are all areas that must be discussed. The answers to these and other questions require systematic and involved planning on the part of both teacher and students. Invariably, some plans will be rejected after they have been proposed. Indeed, the negotiation of the rejected and the accepted strategies is an important aspect of an interdisciplinary study. Such negotiations require all participants to think about the nature and quality of the suggestions made and then to project the consequences of various lines of thought and investigations. Interdisciplinary studies provide valuable opportunities for such activities.

6. *Cooperative Investigations* Interdisciplinary studies are intrinsically cooperative. An investigation is never successful without effective planning, coordination, and cooperative input from the participants.

A significant amount of research has been conducted on the impact of cooperative learning on student achievement, motivation, and attitude in virtually all subject areas. In general, the results provide impressive support for the use of cooperative activities in a wide variety of settings, including interdisciplinary investigations. Prominent researchers in this area (Johnson & Johnson, 1993) suggest three different goal structures: cooperative, individualistic, and competitive. They decry the degree to which competition pervades the school environment. While acknowledging that competition and individual approaches have a place within the school setting, these researchers suggest a dramatic shift from traditionally competitive to more-cooperative situations. Clearly, children must learn to deal effectively with others. Schools can and should provide such opportunities for such learning to all children. Interdisciplinary methods provide the context within which that cooperation can thrive.

CONDITIONS NECESSARY FOR INTERDISCIPLINARY TEACHING

Interdisciplinary teaching should perhaps be called *interdisciplinary learning,* because the role of the teacher is that of facilitator. The teacher so orchestrates the unit that children know what they are going to do, what everyone in the class is trying to learn, and how they should begin. The conditions necessary for interdisciplinary teaching are illustrated in Figure 1.4 and described in the following paragraphs.

Communication

Before the unit begins, especially if it is a first try at an interdisciplinary approach, there must be good communication. The principal and your colleagues need to know what you are planning to try and why you think this approach will broaden children's skills and experiences. Parents need to know that their children will be studying the broad topic that you select, and that from time to time their children may need help, suggestions, and even supplies from home. Moreover, it is always helpful when parents talk about and pose questions related to the unit's theme. A sample letter to parents is provided in Appendix A-XIV.

For a variety of reasons, new teaching methods make their way slowly into the curriculum. Nevertheless, all teachers need to look for instructional methodologies that will involve children, enhance learning, and increase student interest.

Preparation

The successful teacher knows that each lesson must be carefully thought out, procedural notes must be made, instructional materials must be located and made ready, and finally, children must be motivated and mentally prepared to undertake a new series of lessons. As the lessons proceed, the teacher must keep some records of children's performance and notes regarding the "workability" of the several parts of each lesson. A series of successful

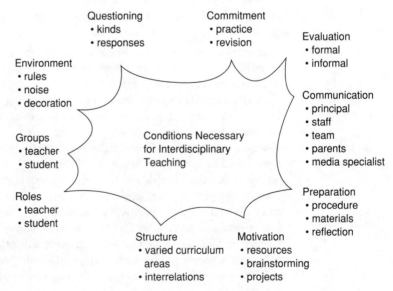

FIGURE 1.4
Conditions necessary for interdisciplinary teaching

lessons is the result of time invested, care in planning, and the keeping of accurate, ongoing records.

The need to rethink a lesson after it has been taught is important. The teacher can detect strengths, weaknesses, and needs related to both instructional methodology and particular children. Rethinking a lesson readies the teacher for the next day, tunes the teacher in to the needs of specific children, and provides the means by which to modify subsequent lessons.

Motivation

Once the topic or theme has been selected, it is important to set the stage. You might want to develop an interactive bulletin board relating to the theme. Bulletin boards that actively involve children are an effective means of provoking thought. Time should be set aside during the day for small groups of learners to work on the bulletin board together.

A trip to the library or resource center, or a library story about the theme, will familiarize children with a variety of sources of information that they will be able to use. You also may wish to use a filmstrip or videotape, arrange a field trip, or explore an Internet connection.

As the unit begins, children are involved in brainstorming, interacting with adults, and bringing items to school. Perhaps a parent would be willing to share personal experiences related to the theme. Another person may have artifacts to share or a job related to the theme. A letter sent home in advance can alert the people involved about your needs.

Once interest is high, you are ready to continue. Converse with the children about things that they know or have found out about the topic. You might ask, "What are some things you already know or would like to know about the theme?" Accept all contributions. Write them on an overhead transparency, a flip chart, or newsprint so you can refer to their ideas later. Gather as many ideas as possible. You can then have the students group their ideas, or you can do it. At the beginning of the next lesson, display the headings with subtopics on the board and ask the children to each make a first, second, and third choice of topics that are of interest to them. In this way, you will establish working groups of children with similar interests.

You can use the organized ideas and suggestions of the children along with learning elements that you select to develop. A list of possible group projects should be posted for the students to see.

You will have to help groups organize, plan, and get started. Once the children have completed one or more interdisciplinary units, they will become accustomed to accepting responsibility for direction and discussion, and for making decisions about the assignment of responsibilities to various group members. Each group will need a leader, a recorder, and two or more subtopic leaders. With practice, children will learn to operate fairly independently. They will be able to set many of their own goals, organize their group so it functions effectively, work cooperatively, and support each other in the development of the final unit report or project. The teacher's role is to help children set these goals, organize their group, find information, and make plans; supply the group with needed materials, supplies, and resources; and show them how to find important documents and how to plan and write reports or complete other projects.

You will stimulate interest and involvement during the development of a theme by combining skills and concepts from several disciplines. Explore the many possible avenues for individual and group investigation. Such a diversified approach can develop interest in and

motivation for reading, and foster a need for developing planning skills. An equally important lesson is the value of personal success through planning and cooperative activities.

Structure

A truly interdisciplinary unit contains elements from several traditional content areas. If
you spend a few minutes thinking and jotting down ideas, you will be able to develop narrowly focused subtopics in each of the several disciplines for each group of children. Ask
yourself what about the topic might lend itself to the development of an arithmetic concept,
for example. Either at the designated time for the interdisciplinary unit or at another time
during the day, you also can use music lessons to focus on the theme. Choose songs related
to the theme; read them and ask children to listen carefully to the lyrics. Ask them such
questions as "Are there words frequently associated with the theme?" and "Do these words
make you think of any special things about the theme?"

As the interdisciplinary unit draws to a close, help children look for interrelationships:
"How did the arithmetic help us to better understand the theme?" "What other things did
we learn from the songs we listened to during the unit?" You can use your broad knowledge
base to help children focus on how arithmetic and music have deepened the group's understanding of the theme.

Roles

One of the unique characteristics of an interdisciplinary unit is that new learning and teaching
roles emerge. The transition is not rapid, for either the children or the teacher. It usually takes
two or three short units for both the teacher and the children to acclimate themselves to their
new roles. The teacher's role slowly shifts from lecturer, presenter, and programmer to facilitator, one who makes something happen. The teacher shows children in small groups how to
organize, plan, assign tasks, and collate, organize, and present information. These skills are part
of what children learn when they participate in an interdisciplinary unit. Like all other learning, these skills take time and practice to acquire. Their acquisition also requires that the teacher
relinquish certain roles that may be ingrained and almost automatic. One method that is effective in helping teachers consciously change their behavior from that of lecturer to that of facilitator is called *wait-time*. This is a questioning strategy in which the teacher is asked to (1) wait
at least 3 seconds after asking a question, or better still, wait patiently until the question has
been answered, (2) refrain from rephrasing or repeating the child's answer, and (3) wait after
one child has responded to be sure that other children with responses have a chance to be heard.
This would seem to be an easy behavioral change to make. Unfortunately, however, this is not
usually the case. It is so much easier to say "Do it this way" than it is to say "Does anyone have
an idea about how we might do this?" and then wait for as many responses as are forthcoming.
But with practice using a tape recorder, and sometimes with the help of a colleague with a
watch, these behavioral changes can be made and slowly become automatic. This is true in general of shifting the teaching role to one of facilitator.

Groups

Once the interdisciplinary unit is underway, you, the teacher, *must* make sure that every
child in every group understands what the group's task is, what he or she is supposed to do,
and with whom he or she is supposed to work. This can be accomplished by using a simple

NAME_____

Our group is learning

about _____

My job is to find out about

_____

I am working with _____

_____

FIGURE 1.5
Sample questionnaire card

questionnaire in the form of a card for each child. Distribute the cards at each table while asking that each child stop, complete the card, and then go back to work. You might use a card like the one shown in Figure 1.5. You can go through the cards quickly to identify the children who need additional explanations and help in getting started.

Interdisciplinary learning focuses on the learning dynamics within groups and how groups can enhance each participant's mastery level. The group must see that each group member knows what the group is is supposed to do, and what, collectively, the group has learned. This requires intergroup tutoring, which is enforced by the teacher. The teacher directs questions about what the group has learned to an individual member. Then, each member of the group receives the score (representing the level of task mastery) that the individual who is called on generates. In no time, each group member assumes responsibility for other members because they all know that individual success may be dependent on the success of coworkers.

Environment

The teacher who is most comfortable when in control needs to make several substantial adjustments. First, the teacher must slowly and honestly relinquish control to the working groups. At the same time, the teacher must go over with the children a short list of rules and expectations. These might include "Work quietly so as not to disturb other groups," "Only one person at a time may leave a group" (to get needed materials or conference with the teacher), "No one may leave the room without permission," and so on. The teacher also must make provisions for necessary visits to the library and resource center, and for field trips.

It is wise to expect that the groups will be noisy sometimes, especially when they are working on their first few units. When this happens, move quickly to the group and make sure that each member is on task.

During the course of an interdisciplinary unit, the experienced teacher transfers control to groups only as quickly as the group's responsibility and capacity for self-management develop. Children will probably never manage themselves as quietly and as efficiently as adults, or as adults wish they would. Indeed, the learning process itself helps children to be self-starters and self-managers.

The discussion thus far has related to slow transfer of management responsibilities from the teacher to the groups. Each group of children working together and setting their own goals should develop its own rules for acceptable behavior. And what a wonderful day it is when you, the teacher, can stand back and watch five or six groups of children planning and working cooperatively together toward a common goal, all the time exercising reasonable self-management.

Working groups will be teacher-dependent in the beginning. If there are six groups working, however, the teacher will be able to spend no more than 8 or 10 minutes with each group in an hour. To the teacher, this will appear to occupy all the time during the hour; to the individual children, it will appear that they are being neglected for five-sixths of the time. It is important to explain this phenomenon to the children and, at least for the first few days, to keep a record of time spend with each group. This assures the teacher that no single group is unfairly monopolizing time and allows the teacher to refer to the record when assuring groups that they are all being visited.

A second environmental problem relates to level of classroom noise. While some educators make a distinction between constructive and destructive noise, in truth, all noise beyond a certain level is antithetic to productive thought, concentration, and work. At the same time, the noise level may affect the teacher and children differently. Before taking steps to lower the noise level, begin by asking children what their perceptions are. You might say, "Some of the children think the room is a bit noisy. They say that they are having a hard time concentrating. What do you think about the noise level right now?" Then listen carefully. Generally, children are painfully honest. If they think the noise level is appropriate (and it is not distracting another class), then it probably is appropriate for them. You cannot set an interdisciplinary unit into operation and honestly expect children to plan and work together in an environment where you can hear a pin drop. Keep in mind, too, that your behavior is as strong a guide to classroom decorum as are your words. If you go directly to the working group of children who are making more than the acceptable level of noise, get close to the group, and speak very quietly, the immediate effect will be to lower the noise level at the table. Have you ever shown a film in a darkened room and noticed that when you turned up the sound, the children too, get noisier? And when you turned down the sound, the room noise decreased? Your quiet voice, spoken directly to the noisy group, is far more effective than a warning shouted across the room!

Lastly, the classroom decoration, which in the past has been designed and installed only by the teacher, will give way to group reports developed by children in their quest for knowledge. Posters, displays, collections, booklets, and pictures are but a few of the tangible things that children will develop as they seek to satisfy the challenge of their particular unit segment. Whatever form these documents take, they must be the very best quality of work that the children can do. If you have a classroom computer with a printer, you may require that at least part of the work be completed on the word processing program. You should have dictionaries and hand-held calculators available so that children can check their spelling and arithmetic. When so many critics today are delivering the "can't read, can't write, can't spell, can't solve problems" liturgy, what better way to enhance those very skills than to place a requirement of high quality on the group and their reporting documents? It is up to the teacher to set the standards and encourage children to meet them, and once they have been met, to praise the quality, precision, and accuracy of their products. Positive reinforcement works. Why not build a system in which children can learn and be reinforced at the same time?

Questioning

Questions facilitate information sharing. As a teacher, you want information about the thinking that children are doing, the conclusions that they are making, and the logical mental structures that they are building. Children, in turn, want to know when, why, and where. To understand the art of asking questions, a bit of situational classification helps. What kind of an answer are you expecting? Questions often can be divided into two categories: those that can and those that cannot be answered. Questions that can be answered fall into two subgroups: those designed to elicit a desired answer and those that are genuine information seekers or sharers.

If our questioning strategy can begin as one that frames questions intended to assess a child's understanding of a particular idea or concept, then questions become a powerful methodological adjunct. Inquiry, investigation, and discovery—strategies that are used continuously in interdisciplinary units—require that the teacher ask many questions. Questions alternated with further investigations serve to focus and move the activities toward desired understanding. Your objectives serve as organizers for your questions.

It is important to note that children are not very good at framing questions, and the teacher may need to help the children clarify meaning before proceeding. You need to consider at least three possible kinds of answers to a question: a direct answer, a reference to a source of information, and a possible procedure to find a useful answer. We can unconsciously condition children to expect a teacher to always provide the answers. Yet when dealing with investigations and processes common to all areas of the curriculum, meaningful answers may require considerable investigation.

Evaluation

Formal and informal evaluation must both be considered when developing thematic units. Multiple-choice, true/false, short-answer, and essay tests can all be a part of your plan. Informal evaluation is also important. Thematic units provide numerous opportunities for the development of portfolios. Checklists, anecdotal records, videotapes, "I learned" statements, and reflection are only a few of the many informal evaluation techniques appropriate for thematic units. A variety of informal evaluation techniques have been included with each sample unit in Chapter 3.

Interdisciplinary studies demand a variety of summarizing or reporting procedures designed so that groups of children can tell the others working on related parts of the study what they are doing and what they have found out. One teacher might have children put their work on display and schedule time for all children to study the displays. A second teacher might ask students to prepare written reports bound into booklets and to make them a part of the classroom resource center. A third teacher might have students publish a research report that contains summaries of the activities of individuals and participating groups.

In every case, the reports, displays, and booklets should be accepted by the teachers only if they are judged to be of good quality and representative of careful thought and effort. You may wish to try any one or all of these reporting techniques. Regardless of what is selected, you will discover that the quality of children's work and the learning progress they make are closely correlated with your expectations for careful, neat, quality products representing the best (in your judgment) that the child or group of children can deliver. The following relates to displays of projects but could apply equally well to other information-sharing procedures.

Display develops pride and self-assurance on the part of the students involved as well as providing information for the observer. It follows that materials displayed should be judged to be among the best work produced. If anything the child produces is displayed without consideration of quality, the whole procedure loses credibility and validity in the eyes of the children and they will be less likely to put forth their best effort in the future. You should encourage editing, emphasizing the need for clear sentences and legible writing. You will find that planning for a formal display of the results of student investigations is an important factor in motivation.

Let us now consider the test trap. It goes like this: *We* want to know whether children are learning. *Parents* want to know whether their children are learning. *Children* want to know whether they are learning. So we sample parts of the unit and write some test items or some desired behaviors. Then we give the test or make the observations. If children miss certain items, we feel duty bound to go back and review that section of the unit. Then it occurs to us that we can avoid the review altogether if we use the test items or desired behaviors to suggest where we should place the teaching emphasis. We are now focusing our teaching on the test, and it works! It works so well that we may forget how important *all* of the activities in the unit are for concept formation.

We are all under pressure to rank children and compare their learning accomplishments. In doing this, however, we sometimes forget that children are different and that lesson quality varies considerably from day to day.

Administrators, parents, and teachers view testing differently. Teachers are concerned with learning differences and individual progress of children in their room. Administrators may be more interested in mean score differences from room to room and building to building. Parents hold a dual view, one focusing on the needs of a single child, the other seeing the school as a low-budget conveyor of basic skills.

The most important thing a teacher can do to affect learning is to recognize and teach to the abilities and needs of each child. This implies that minimum outcomes are expected and that differences in abilities within classrooms call for a variety of teaching styles and learning tasks.

If you develop a variety of activities to challenge the more-able children into side explorations while keeping the seemingly less-able children involved, all children will accomplish the minimum desired objectives. Some will complete the minimum task and will branch out into self-selected investigations. Such individualization demands flexible teacher evaluation procedures.

Children will learn many facts, skills, and concepts in the course of an interdisciplinary study. In each step, you are asking children to

- gain basic knowledge
- learn to make judgments and choices
- sense the values that come from active learning
- be able to extract from a learning activity useful, lifelong skills, concepts, and values
- inquire into problems, social systems, and natural patterns
- learn the need for patience, care, and repetition
- build a willingness to take risks that carry with them the chance of failure
- generate from one system a set of principles, rules, and concepts that have multiple applications

FIGURE 1.6

Generalized master plan* matrix

COGNITIVE DOMAIN OBJECTIVES†	LANGUAGE ARTS	SCIENCE	SOCIAL STUDIES	MATHEMATICS	OTHERS
1. Observing	X				
2. Recording		X			
3. Describing					
4. Defining					
5. Measuring					
6. Posing questions					
7. Synthesizing					
8. Hypothesizing			X		
9. Inferring					
10. Predicting				X	
11. Generalizing					
12. Evaluating					
13. Verifying					
AFFECTIVE DOMAIN OBJECTIVES†					
1. Functioning independently					
2. Functioning effectively with others					
3. Developing and holding a set of values					

*The four marked intersections are used to illustrate the development of desired behavior statements.

†These objectives are general: there is no list of subparts.

At the beginning of a thematic unit, we need to find out what children know about the theme. We need this information so we don't lose valuable instructional time, and so we can incorporate activities for all children, small groups, and even a single child after being assured that needed prerequisite skills are present. We then need to find out what children have learned as the unit is being taught and when the unit is complete.

Since children are not always able to express what they know through language, it is useful to behavioralize some of the desired learning outcomes. Language coupled with activity enhances both language skills and the child's acquisition of concepts. It becomes important to ask children to explain and at the same time to demonstrate understanding through showing, manipulating, and drawing pictures. Test items and behavior statements get at the same information.

Figure 1.6 is a generalized year's plan for concept development. Each intersection on the matrix represents an objective to be gained in one subject area. Four intersections have been marked. These four will be used to illustrate the development of desired behavior statements. Begin with "The child will be able to ____1____, ____2____." On line 1 insert a verb such as *tell, write, explain, point to, connect, reverse, sort,* and so on. On line 2 describe what you expect the child to do to satisfy the objective. For example:

1. Intersection of Observing and Language Arts: The child will be able to connect events in a play to those in its corresponding story in printed form.

2. Intersection of Recording and Science: The child will be able to record results of plant growth over time in tabular, graphical, and paragraph form.

3. Intersection of Hypothesizing and Social Studies: The child will be able to explain cause and effect in situations relating to the Thanksgiving feast following the pilgrims' first winter in the New World.

4. Intersection of Predicting and Mathematics: The child will be able to predict the overall relationship (π) between a circle's circumference and its diameter given string, a measuring device, and a set of circular objects to be measured.

As a teacher, you need a variety of diagnostic tools. Learning needs fall in the motor, cognitive, and affective domains. The following collection is intended to suggest a number of ways you can gather information.

Peer Perception Statements. Sociograms can promote effective social interrelationships and help to identify those needing intervention. If each child is asked to supply the names of two other children with whom he or she would like to work, the number of times each child is selected gives some information about peer perception and insight into effective grouping. If you use a roster and tally the number of times each child is selected, this will give you a quick ranking of children in terms of peer perception specific to the task.

A somewhat more elaborate space-diagram can be developed that will identify natural, cooperative working groups.

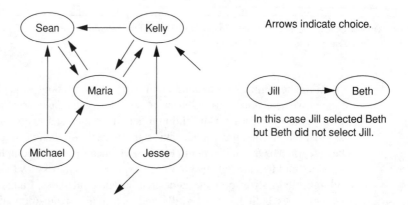

Such a diagram will help to identify potential leaders and children who are frequently excluded.

Priority Statements. The children's ranking by preference of subjects will help you choose interesting instructional activities, and it will also measurably aid in grouping children for different thematic investigations. A sample priority list follows.

Mark 1 by the thing you would choose first. Mark the other items 2, 3, 4, and so on, showing your second, third, and fourth choices.

_____ Looking at pictures

_____ Using the computer

_____ Listening to stories

_____ Writing a poem

_____ Drawing pictures

_____ Watching movies

Feeling Statements. You can gather information that will help you understand emotional problems about children's feelings by asking children to complete statements such as the following:

When I work with my building team I _____

When someone does all the talking I _____

I wish the group leader would _____

Sometimes I feel unhappy because _____

The information you gain is valid only if you have established a sound level of trust with the children. Interest, feelings, and understandings can also be understood through the use of a variety of assessments, which can be given at regular intervals.

"I Learned" Statements. A list of "I" learned items created by the children helps you assess their understanding of the purposes and objectives of the theme.

When I was _____ I learned _____

Many teachers have found that a two-way chart, shown in Figure 1.7, is a simple way to keep records of pupil progress. It will provide you with daily information about how each child is progressing and how well each part of the lesson is working. You will notice that your previous behavioral statements are repeated. As the thematic unit progresses, you can add additional behaviors or you can start a new chart. Some teachers have found that the chart can be cumbersome if too many behaviors are used at one time. In practice, you will find that if you select two or three behaviors and about one-third of the children per day to observe, the chart won't interfere with your work with children. In fact, some teachers have observed that it helps them in framing questions and keeping children on task.

When the unit is complete, you can convert the blanks, lines, and crosses into numbers and generate progress estimates of the performance of each child in the class. In addition, the two-way chart is a useful tool when reporting to parents during conferences. The chart enables you to indicate the positive accomplishments of the child and those that will require additional effort. In fact, the chart might suggest ways that parents can work with their children and thus help you in accomplishing objectives.

The marks in the boxes enable you to indicate improvement as the child approaches and accomplishes the objective.

	Can explain why kites fly	Can calculate stick lengths	Can define lift, drag, and bridle	Individual Totals
Jason A.	☐	X	X	4
Nick B.	☐	X	/	3
Alissa G.	/	/	X	4
Kristi F.	X	X	X	6
Carmen J.	/	X	X	5
Greg R.	☐	/	☐	1
Class Totals	4	10	9	

No evidence ☐ 0 points   Some evidence ⊡ 1 point
Good evidence ⊠ 2 points

FIGURE 1.7
Two-way chart

If you do not see any evidence of the desired behavior: ☐

If you see some, but not adequate, evidence: ⊡

If the child's behavior indicates satisfactory accomplishments: ⊠

The numbers at the right side are generated by assigning and adding the separate numbers.

☐ = 0   ⊡ = 1   ⊠ = 2

When you add the columns vertically, you are able to assess the entire class's progress on each of the desired behaviors. Low numbers indicate that a review or a revision may be in order. High numbers indicate that your teaching and the lessons are accomplishing the objectives.

The sample two-way chart could be interpreted as follows:

1. Jason, Nick, and Alissa seem to be working and accomplishing in a satisfactory way.

2. Carmen and Kristi are doing above-average work; you may want to direct them to more-complex investigations of their choice.

3. Greg is having trouble. You may wish to make some careful observations and ask some questions to find out where the problems are. You may have to develop some specific remedial assignments.

4. There is something wrong with the activity intended to develop the first objective. The activity may not have been presented effectively, it may be too difficult, or necessary antecedent skills may be lacking. In any event, a review or additional activities are in order.

Teaching is a complex art form and the teacher, with the children, attempts to create the best learning environment possible. For this to be done well, the progress of each child must be continuously assessed and those lessons or instructional procedures that are ineffective must be replaced with better ones. Learning environments are improved only through careful, systematic evaluation.

Thematic units are challenging, difficult, and often complex. But they do exploit knowledge connections that are natural to children, and they do offer alternatives to a compartmentalized approach. The bridges often prompt new learnings and expand the children's understanding of the interconnections of the elements of the theme.

Commitment

Since it is clear that interdisciplinary methodology is different from a typical, didactic, instructional approach, it stands to reason that a commitment must be made by the teacher to pursue this form of teaching well beyond a single trial unit. In fact, the first unit may require so many minor behavior changes, by both the teacher and the children, that it most likely will be somewhat disappointing. It would be far better to plan a series of several units and begin with very brief ones. These might be considered practice units in which teacher techniques and student expectations and understandings can be put into place. Slowly, as success grows, the duration of the units can be expanded to fit the needs of the topic and the level of interest of the children.

PROS AND CONS OF INTERDISCIPLINARY METHODS

If you are asked about interdisciplinary methods or the thematic unit approach, the questioner will probably want to know your opinion about the merits of this kind of teaching and learning. In most cases, pros and cons are based on a set of evaluative criteria. It is, then, your task to describe just what it is that you want the instructional program to do and what it is that you want children to accomplish. Key points, in addition to defining the purpose of instruction, include the needs that children have to be successful, to reach established goals, and to be fairly rewarded. There are many elements that motivate children to learn. Not only is extrinsic reward (good grades and peer approval) important, but also, what children willingly learn must be interesting, challenging, and often puzzling. It is difficult to look at a lesson and know whether it will appeal to children. Often, the lesson must first be tried with children before this can be determined. Once you are able to describe what you want children to accomplish and determine how effectively the lessons you are using function as this element in the learning process, you are well on your way to discussing the pros and cons of interdisciplinary approaches.

One of the strengths of interdisciplinary instruction is that it helps children make connections and see relationships beyond those possible in a curriculum designed around separate disciplines. A second strength is that once we come to believe that learning is the coming together of children, replete with their many needs, within a rich, stimulating, and organized environment and with a challenge to try, to find out, and to understand, then we can assign with confidence parts of the day to interdisciplinary investigations. As we continue to examine interdisciplinary units, it quickly becomes clear that they involve a group process by the children and thus require a substantial amount of materials, take more classroom time to complete, generate more interactions in the classroom, and may well take more time to prepare than other approaches. Teachers will find that directions need to be given and posted. But they also will find that many of the learning objectives that they have checked have been accomplished, and that a real atmosphere of classroom trust will have developed.

We asked 250 elementary and middle school teachers in Chicago, Minneapolis, and Seattle who had tried a number of thematic units to respond to the question "What are the

TABLE 1.1
Selected teachers' experience with interdisciplinary methods

Pros	Cons
• improves research skills	• needs flexibility of time
• fun	• takes extra planning to get started
• provides for all levels of learning	• need to try it to decide whether it works
• easy to integrate all areas of the curriculum	• needs more than one try
• involves all learning styles	• materials not always commercially available in needed format
• uses inquiry process	• takes longer
• high interest	• noise level higher
• builds group trust	*•
• easy to be successful for students	•
• group process is clear	•
• easy to evaluate outcomes	
• makes clear connections	
• children are directly involved in the total procedure	
• nonthreatening	
• meaningful content	
*•	
•	
•	

*Your reactions

pros and cons of interdisciplinary methods?" Their responses are listed in Table 1.1. You will notice that the lists of pros and cons differ in both number and direction. The pros tend to be student-oriented gains, and the cons often relate to increased teacher effort. The latter decreases with experience. Once you have tried one or more units, we hope you will add your comments to this list.

IN SUMMARY

Interdisciplinary methods enable the teacher to develop units that focus both on topics of immediate interest to children and on elements that help children come to understand that knowledge and its application are not bounded by traditional curriculum divisions. This is not to suggest that schools abandon the traditional educational structures and develop in their place a totally interdisciplinary curriculum; the problems involved in undertaking such a move would prove to be enormous and overwhelming. We do suggest that an interdisciplinary approach to teaching and learning be accorded a portion of the school day. It is simply not true that basic skills are all that children need to prepare them for a very uncertain future. The individuals who are successful in coping with tomorrow's society and its problems will be those who can cope with new and unfamiliar situations in an understanding and creative manner. What better preparation for future citizens than to involve them in such activities during the formal school day? One or two afternoons a week is a reasonable goal in the beginning. More time is appropriate as the teacher and children become more familiar with the new organizational format.

How many times will you have to work with groups that are involved in an interdisciplinary study, helping them set and work toward goals? Many, to say the least. Most children have been used to working independently, often in competition with others. Working in groups toward group goals will be a new experience for most. Fortunately, they will soon make the transition and not only will work well in groups, but also, if past experiences are any indicators, will become more productive, achieve more, and develop better attitudes. And, perhaps of equal importance, many children who are shy, reserved, and rarely speak up in a traditional classroom format will begin to shine and participate and often take the lead in achieving group goals.

Any classroom in an elementary or middle school will do, as long as it can accommodate working groups. As you progress through several interdisciplinary units, you will have a great deal of child-developed materials to display. Extra shelves and bulletin boards will come in handy. But the single most important, even critical element in interdisciplinary teaching is the shift in roles of teacher and students. The teacher no longer runs the instructional program. The teacher is a planner and facilitator based on all his or her methods classes. The teacher organizes, assembles, and orchestrates the lessons so that children in groups take over much of the responsibility for their own learning. In addition to content, which is clearly the focus of interdisciplinary units, children learn to plan, set goals, delegate responsibility, and bring together a document that represents their very best work as well as a summary of the many things they have learned. All of these are the goals and the outcomes of successful interdisciplinary methods. A list of resources relating to interdisciplinary methods and the thematic unit approach follows. In Chapter 2, we will help you plan your first unit.

Before we begin, however, it is important to establish that interdisciplinary studies is not just another educational fad that is likely to disappear in the short run. As you will see in the following section, interdisciplinary studies is firmly grounded in both experience and sound educational and pegagogical theory.

SITUATING INTERDISCIPLINARY STUDIES WITHIN THE CONSTRUCTIVIST FRAMEWORK

Interdisciplinary studies can be squarely placed with the philosophical position that contends that knowledge cannot be transferred directly from one individual to another. This position holds that knowledge is personal in nature and must be created by each individual through his or her own activity. Such activity in conjunction with peers results in an internalization of ideas and the construction of a personalized form of knowledge.

This contemporary offshoot of cognitive learning theories is known as constructivism. There is ongoing debate about its underlying assumptions and its applicability to the classroom situation given the personal and social nature of knowledge construction. One issue concerns the large-group structure of most classrooms. Constructivism in any of its many forms recognizes the importance of the individual and group in the overall learning process and, to varying degrees, the important influence of the social milieu on the individual's construction of knowledge. Much of the current debate relates to the degree of influence that the social setting has on this constructive activity. The range of views regarding the impact of social setting on construction of knowledge is described by Latour (1992):

> A radical is someone who claims that scientific knowledge is entirely constructed out of social relations; a progressive is someone who would say that it is partially constructed out of social relations but that nature somehow "leaks in" at the end. At the other side of this tug of war, a reactionary is someone who would claim science becomes really scientific only when it finally sheds any trace of social construction; while a conservative would say that although science escapes from society there are still factors from society that "leak in" and influence its development. In the middle would be the marsh of wishy-washy scholars who add a little bit of nature to a little bit of society and shun the two extremes. (p. 276)

One glimpses the nature of some of the disagreement currently surrounding the constructivist position, although all of these positions fall under the single umbrella of constructivism. Regardless of the outcome of the debate on the role of social setting, the importance of genuine student involvement in the learning process is embraced by each of these positions.

This tenet sounds very much like a modern perspective of some of the work of Jean Piaget, Lev Vygotsky, and John Dewey. An early philosopher of education from the University of Chicago, John Dewey was a long-time advocate of the use of activity methods in the classroom. Dewey (1902, 1910) viewed students as potential knowers actively engaged in their own intellectual development rather than as passive receptacles, as did proponents of a position related to the earlier *tabula rasa* perspective, in which students' minds were viewed as blank slates to be written upon at will by teachers and others. Dewey assigned the highest priority in education to important ideas developed within the academic disciplines. His position has been described (Prawat, 1995) as idea-based social constructivism:

> The teacher's task, according to this view, is to create discourse communities to allow students to hammer out and apply the ideas, like the author's point of view in literature, or part-whole relations in mathematics, to real-world phenomena that they can then view with fresh eyes. Ideally in this scenario, the classroom becomes a center of lively discourse where people engage in animated conversations about important intellectual matters. To quote one eighth grade teacher who approached this ideal, "The classroom takes on the characteristics of the 'dining room table' where students converse about books and poems." (p. 20)

Jean Piaget's monumental work was developed over a period of fifty productive years and provides perhaps the most comprehensive framework within which such an activity-oriented curriculum might develop. Central to Piaget's (1973) position was the need for active student involvement in the learning process. In his famous stages of intellectual development he described students' growing ability to develop progressively more abstract concepts based on simpler, more concrete systems. Although Piaget's work has been acutely scrutinized over the past two decades, the basic structure of his work remains essentially intact. This structure can also be viewed as a theoretical foundation supporting more modern constructivist positions. In a similar vein, Lochhead (1985) suggests the following:

> What I see as critical to the new cognitive science is the recognition that knowledge is not an entity that can be simply transferred from those who have it to those who don't. . . . Knowledge is something that each individual learner must construct for and by himself. This view of knowledge as an individual construction . . . is usually referred to as constructivism.

Constructivists make a distinction between information and knowledge. Information can be given or easily transmitted through telling; information is all that is necessary to achieve correct performance. Thus when the purpose of instruction is to transmit information and to get correct performance, explanations do nicely; however, knowledge is not something that can simply be transmitted or given. Gaining knowledge means gaining expertise. Constructivists take the position that explanations will not help transform a novice into an expert. In fact, explanations often serve to perpetrate remedial processing tendencies [remedial processing relates to understanding superficial characteristics of a situation or idea without coming to grips with the essence of that idea]. (p. 627)

One of the goals of contemporary education is to increase students' abilities to process, interpret, evaluate, and generalize ever-increasing amounts of information. It's estimated that the sheer amount of knowledge doubles every decade or so and that computer capability doubles every three years. Under such conditions, it is no wonder that educators have a significant task in simply helping students to identify what is essential, what is desirable, and what is forgettable. Students need to have experiences while they're in school relating to the accessing, manipulation, and understanding of large quantities of information. It has been argued that this skill is and will be more important than student acquisition of specific knowledge. It is certain that much of a student's adult intellectual life will be spent processing information in various ways. The *tabula rasa* view of the mind as a blank slate was never an adequate description, but it is even less appropriate today. The amassing of specific knowledge is becoming less and less important as larger amounts of knowledge are made more accessible to virtually everyone through numerous publications and the WorldWide Web. The Web brings much of the world's knowledge and experience to an individual classroom or home. Many students today have access to the Internet. Thus, it is critical that students begin the process of deciding which knowledge is important, which knowledge is less so, and which information should be disregarded. The problem with real-world problem solving relates to the fact that there is usually too much information rather than not enough. Students must also find ways to access knowledge, gather related ideas from a wide variety of sources, and form their findings into a coherent entity. Interdisciplinary studies has as its very core the development of such information processing skills and abilities. Piaget (1973) has verbalized these ideas as follows:

To understand is to discover. . . . A student who achieves a certain knowledge through free investigation and spontaneous effort will later be able to retain it: He will have acquired a methodology that will serve him for the rest of his life, which will stimulate his curiosity without the risk of exhausting it. At the very least, instead of having his memory take priority over his reasoning power . . . he will learn to make his reason function by himself and learn to build his own ideas freely. The goal of intellectual education is not to know how to repeat or retain ready-made truths. It is in learning to master the truth by oneself at the risk of losing a lot of time in going through all the roundabout ways that are inherent in real activity.

In a very real sense the experts are in agreement about the way in which students will more ably develop relevant and appropriate intellectual structures. Decades ago, cognitive psychologists and educational philosophers provided the theoretical framework within which modern-day constructivism resides. Much of that discussion related to the evolving nature of human intelligence. The implications for schooling are substantial and far reaching. In the following section, we discuss several interpretations of human intelligence and how these newer interpretations relate to interdisciplinary studies.

INTERDISCIPLINARY APPROACHES AND THE NATURE OF HUMAN INTELLIGENCE

Howard Gardner also endorsed Dewey's emphasis on student self-pacing, hands-on activities, and cooperative discourse. Gardner's classic book, *The Frames of Mind: The Theory of Multiple Intelligences* (1978), criticizes the conception of intelligence as a unidimensional variable that can be assigned a number based on a series of intelligence tests. Gardner's theory of multiple intelligences represents a formal assault on the century-old concept of intelligence, particularly as intelligence came to be operationally defined through the idea of the intelligence quotient (IQ). It is Gardner's thesis that intelligence as measured by traditional IQ tests is simply too narrowly conceived.

The idea of multiple contributors to human intelligence is not new. In the 1930s, L. L. Thurstone listed seven factors that he claimed made up general intelligence. The factors were so highly correlated, however, that one could not argue that they were in fact separate. Later, in the 1950s, J. P. Guilford partitioned general intelligence into 180 specific abilities, which he classified under three headings: logical processes, the kinds of information processed, and the products of such processing. Guilford's work does present a kind of theory of multiple intelligences in that he broadened our sense of what the term means to include social judgment (i.e., our judgment of the behavior of others) and creativity, or what is often called divergent thinking. From the teacher's practical point of view, however, Guilford's model is probably too complex and arcane to lend itself to instructional settings.

Through his work as codirector of Project Zero at Harvard University, Gardner proposed a theory of multiple intelligences. He concluded that there are at least seven distinct kinds of intelligence. He called these *linguistic, spatial, logical-mathematical, bodily-kinesthetic, musical, intrapersonal,* and *interpersonal* intelligences. Gardner arrived at his conclusions on the basis of a study of the neurological functions of the brain. He noticed, for example, that people who had suffered strokes or damaged a certain part of the brain could still perform other functions. He also noted that people who are outstanding in one particular form are not necessarily so in others. Thus, he was able to take the argument further than Thurstone, who could not show unrelated abilities.

A common argument to counter Gardner's theory is that musical abilities, athletic skills, and so on are talents rather than forms of intelligence. Gardner went to great lengths to establish criteria by which to measure whether a particular ability, say in music, was merely a talent or was actually a form of intelligence. According to Gardner, for an ability to qualify as an intelligence it must have a developmental feature, be found in special populations such as geniuses or virtuosos, provide some evidence of localization in the brain, and support a symbolic or notational system. Gardner's theory remains controversial in spite of the widespread support of well wishers who want desperately to believe that everyone is highly intelligent albeit in different ways.

Gardner's work gives a boost to advocates of interdisciplinary teaching and learning. If Gardner is right in saying that each of us is genetically endowed with particular forms of intelligence (while acknowledging that all humans have all the forms to varying degrees), then the project activity/constructivist approach so closely identified with interdisciplinary efforts provides a niche for all learners. Although Gardner described only seven types of intelligence, he also suggested that other forms probably exist, opening the door even wider for learners.

The application of Gardner's theory to social settings is typically not so rigid that students learn only in the area of their apparent strengths but instead are stretched to work in those areas in which they might be deficient as well. The point is that if these seven realms are important, then students should be involved in exploring them. This opens the curriculum as well as the modes of learning considerably. Because interdisciplinary teaching and learning tend to focus not on separate disciplines but on broader themes, the potential to engage most or all of the seven types of intelligence is much greater than it would be in a traditional setting.

Although Gardner's work is not accepted unconditionally by psychologists, his ideas have had great influence on teachers in school settings. His work seems to have struck a genuinely responsive chord with many educators, particularly those who advocate interdisciplinary teaching and learning. More than anything else, the seven types of intelligence give teachers and students a goal structure within which to work, one that is far more liberating than the traditional sense of intelligence as being related primarily to knowledge acquisition. Gardner's courageous attempt to redefine intelligence to include abilities beyond the typical paper-and-pencil/abstract thought processes, traditionally so valued in schools, remains controversial, and some skeptics have decided already that it is little more than a passing fancy. Time will tell.

In recent times, the work of researchers such as Robert Sternberg at Yale University has taken the concept of intelligence in more of a cognitive direction than Gardner's neurophysical approach would suggest. Sternberg has developed what he calls a triarchic theory of intelligence. His triarchy is composed of contextual intelligence, or the ability to adapt and shape one's environment; experiential intelligence, or the ability to produce new ideas and combine information into meaningful structures; and componential intelligence, or the ability to think abstractly, process information, and make decisions about what one needs to do to accomplish a task. Like Gardner, Sternberg has not produced operational definitions of his construct in the form of standardized instruments that could measure intelligence, so in the meantime, we are left with such familiar and traditional measurement instruments as the Stanford-Binet.

The work of researchers such as Gardner, Sternberg, and others points to the dissatisfaction so many feel with the concept of intelligence. In times past, people were no doubt as wide ranging in their intellectual capacities as they are today, but no one bothered to measure them. Instead, informal judgment was the basis for deciding such matters. Those of us in the teaching profession share a common dream of improving learning for children, and whether all of our attempts to define intelligence have contributed much to that dream is open to continued discussion.

The constructivist framework and the ongoing interest in redefining the nature of human intelligence support the major thesis of this book. That is, children must be actively engaged in the generation and development of their own intellectual structures. Moreover, there is an important social dimension to learning: learning takes place within a social milieu and as such must involve nontrivial interaction with other human beings (Vygotsky). The goal of including thematic investigations as an important component of an individual's intellectual development is, we believe, supported by theoretical as well as practical perspectives. Understanding of specific subject matter (i.e., math, science, social studies, and literature) continues to be an important goal of the school experience. Using interdisciplinary approaches in the elementary and middle school classrooms is more appropriate, more possible, and more defensible than ever before. Interdisciplinary studies will not and should not replace the development of a wide variety of specific understandings in the various disciplines. However, when viewed in conjunction with these specific understandings, interdisciplinary studies can be a valuable part of every child's intellectual, social, and emotional development.

We turn now to considerations relating to the planning and implementation of integrated approaches to the curriculum.

Additional Resources

Brooks, J., & Brooks, H. (1993). *In search of understanding: The case for constructivist classrooms*. Alexandria, VA: ASCD.

Fogarty, R. (1991). *The mindful school: How to integrate the curricula*. Palatine, IL: Skylight Publishing.

Jacobs, H. (1990). *Interdisciplinary curriculum: Design and implementation*. Alexandria, VA: American Association for Curriculum Development.

Johnson, D., & Johnson, R. (1993). *Circles of learning: Cooperation in the classroom* (4th ed.). Edina, MN: Interaction.

National Council of Teachers of Mathematics. (1989). *Curriculum and evaluation standards for school mathematics*. Reston, VA: NCTM.

National Council for the Social Studies. (1994). *Curriculum standards for social studies*. Washington, DC: NCSS.

Shoemaker, B. (1991, June). Education 2000: Integrated curriculum. *Phi Delta Kappan, 793–797*.

Willis, S. (1995, January). Refocusing the curriculum: Making interdisciplinary efforts work. *Education Update, 37*(1).

References

Blais, D. (1988, November). Constructivism: A theoretical revolution for algebra. *Mathematics Teacher, 624–631*.

Dewey, J. (1981). The experimental theory of knowledge. In J. J. McDermott (Ed.), *The philosophy of John Dewey* (pp. 175–193). Chicago: University of Chicago Press.

Dewey, J. (1902). *The child and the curriculum*. Chicago: University of Chicago Press.

Gardner, H. (1991). *The unschooled mind*. New York: Basic Books.

Gardner, H. (1978). *The frames of mind: The theory of multiple intelligences*. New York: Basic Books.

Guilford, J. (1988). Some changes in structure of the intellect model. *Educational and Psychological Measurement, 48*, 1–4.

Latour, B. (1992). One more turn after the social turn. In E. McMullin (Ed.), *The social dimensions of science* (pp. 272–294). Notre Dame, IN: University of Notre Dame Press.

Lockehead, J. (1985). New horizons in educational development. *Review of Research in Education*. Washington, DC: American Educational Research Association.

Phillips, D. C. (1995). The good, the bad, and the ugly: The many faces of constructivism. *Educational Researcher, 24* (7), 5–12.

Piaget, J. (1973). *To understand is to invent*. New York: Grossman.

Prawat, R. (1995, October). Misreading Dewy: Reform, projects and the language game. *Educational Researcher, 24* (7), 13–22.

Sternberg, R. (1990). *Metaphors of mind: Conceptions of the nature of intelligence*. New York: Cambridge University Press.

Vygotsky, L. S. (1978). *Mind in society: The development of higher psychological processes*. (M. Cole, V. John-Steiner, S. Schribner, & E. Souberman, Eds. and Translators) Cambridge, MA: Harvard University Press.

How?
A Methodology of Thematics

A thematic unit begins within the children's environment and expands to include elements of all curricular areas. You, the teacher, use all you have learned about teaching in your methods classes to build the theme around the children's interests and slowly facilitate conceptual development through the challenges you offer, the questions you pose, and the investigations you initiate.

Thematic units can take on a variety of forms. They may be of brief duration or extend over several weeks or more. Most teachers who have tried a thematic unit say it is important to start small. Once you become more experienced you can expand the time devoted to a topic. At first, however, it is crucial that you don't let the new approach overwhelm you.

A unit might center around a narrow theme, such as *sailboats,* or a broader theme, such as *transportation*. It is key to choose a topic of high interest to your class. It is also necessary to consider what the children will learn about the topic as a result of the unit. A thematic unit must be a series of integrated lessons with a clearly defined purpose. Teachers find that as they help children plan and work their way through interdisciplinary studies, they all become more skilled in identifying and developing their own themes.

Once you have identified the theme, you will generate related ideas using a brainstorming process. All curricular areas should be considered during this process, after which specific lessons will evolve. The example given in this chapter has been developed in precisely this way. At first this procedure may seem very complex. However, with a little experience you will be able to make all curricular areas a meaningful part of any thematic unit. Once you have identified the general outline, it is then appropriate for you to continue brainstorming with students. Such experiences give them control over their own destiny and encourage them to utilize their awareness of the related nature of the world around them. In addition, such student involvement will help them to develop a sense of self-direction. Planning continues as objectives are written, activities are defined, and evaluation procedures are selected.

KEY STEPS IN PLANNING A THEMATIC UNIT

To convince you that this is not an impossibly difficult task, we will work through planning a thematic unit.

The steps that we will work through are listed in the following outline.

Key Planning Steps

1. Theme

2. Time

3. Unit Overview

4. Brainstorming

5. Unit Objectives

6. Vocabulary

7. Planning Lessons

   A. Curricular Areas

   B. Learning Styles

   C. Questioning

   D. Inclusion

8. Evaluation

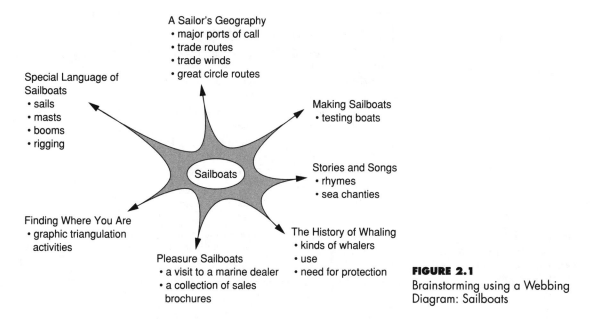

FIGURE 2.1
Brainstorming using a Webbing Diagram: Sailboats

We have selected sailboats as a topic for this unit because it is fairly narrow and also is a segment of the larger theme of transportation.

Theme

As indicated, we have selected a topic for you: sailboats. This topic is narrow in scope and easily developed for a first experience with a thematic unit.

Time

About 2 weeks will be needed to complete this unit. It could be expanded into a longer period of time, but it is best to keep it short the first time.

Unit Overview

Now it is time to identify the broader picture of what we hope to accomplish in this unit. Our stated objective will be that students will design, construct, and test various types of wind-driven craft using activities from a variety of curricular areas.

Brainstorming

The next step is brainstorming, which can be done in several ways. One way is to list topics or ideas, with input from children, that relate to the sailboat theme. After a few minutes of brainstorming you should have a number of ideas. It is essential at this stage that you accept all ideas. One way to do this is to list all suggestions on the board while refraining from judgment at this time. Research has suggested that reinforcing brainstorming too early tends to "turn off" or extinguish many of the children's potential responses. Then you will impose some type of structure on the items that you have generated. No one structure is uniquely correct. Start by putting the word *Sailboats* in the middle of a piece of paper. Then arrange

	Sailboats	
What I **K**now	What I **W**ant to Know	What I **L**earned
Sailing is fun. We have places near our school where there are sailboats being used. You need wind. Sailboats come in many shapes and sizes.	More about the kinds of sailboats. How to make a sailboat. How to make a sailboat go faster. Who uses sailboats? Have people used sailboats for a long time? How do you know where you are if you can't see land?	

FIGURE 2.2

Brainstorming using a **K**now-**W**ant to Know-**L**earned (KWL) Sheet: Sailboats

the ideas that were brainstormed, grouping them according to subtopic, around *Sailboats* so that you form a webbing diagram like the one shown in Figure 2.1. For your future use, a planning sheet that contains a blank webbing diagram is provided in Appendix A-I.

A second method is to have students brainstorm using a KWL data-retrieval sheet like the one shown in Figure 2.2.

Students can work on their sheets alone or in pairs. Begin by asking students what they know (K) about sailboats, then ask them to generate and record their ideas on individual KWL sheets. When they are finished, make a master class list. You may choose to brainstorm as a class instead, using the KWL sheet as a transparency or copying it onto the chalkboard or a flip chart. A blank KWL sheet is provided for your future use in Appendix A-II. It can be made into a transparency or a similar model can be made on a flip chart for ease of future reference.

Repeat the brainstorming procedure, this time having students explore and share what they want (W) to know about sailboats. You can then use this information to impose some type of structure on students' needs. Students should save a copy of the KWL sheet for reference and to examine what they have learned (L) at the conclusion of the unit.

Unit Objectives

Once you have organized the brainstorming ideas into a structure, you will develop your unit objectives. These can be organized as follows.

Students will:

1. become familiar with various kinds of sailboats.

2. learn about various aspects of life aboard a ship that has sails, including procedures for storing food and water, the social organization of ships, and the various duties of sailors.

3. learn and listen to traditional songs of the sea.

4. design and decorate one or more sailboats.

5. be able to explain how the various parts of a sailboat work together to redirect the force of the wind so the boat can sail in many directions.

6. prepare a portfolio of all activity materials and keep a journal of individual activity experiences.

7. participate in a model-sailboat regatta (race).

A blank unit objectives sheet for your future use is provided in Appendix A-III.

Vocabulary

Before you begin to plan specific lessons, you should identify key vocabulary words to be developed. We have identified the following as vocabulary words to be developed for the sailboat theme.

Vocabulary

hull

resistance

boom

mast

port

starboard

regatta

A blank planning sheet for vocabulary words is provided in Appendix A-IV.

Planning Lessons

Now that you have identified objectives and vocabulary words for the unit, you can begin to organize your lessons. Activities should be developed to meet the needs of learners in your class. The following eight activities have been developed for use with the sailboat theme. Following those are ten additional activities to be used for extension or evaluation. A blank activity planning sheet is provided in Appendix A-V.

ACTIVITY ONE

Sailboat Introduction

Objective: to introduce the class to the sailboat topic

Materials: a videotape, filmstrip, or book depicting sailboats (consult your school or public library listings)

Procedure: Show the class one or more videotapes or filmstrips, or read to the class one or more books about sailboats. After the class has viewed the video or filmstrip, or read the book, lead students in a discussion. This discussion ultimately should lead to a recognition by the class that they need to know more about sailboats.

Evaluation: active participation in the discussion

ACTIVITY TWO

Research Center Search

Objective: to help each student locate books related to sailing and to provide time for students to read them

Materials: library books

Procedure: Help the children find library books about sailboats and sailing, then allow time for reading. Let them know that they will later be asked to discuss what they have learned from the books.

To save time, you may wish to check ahead with your librarian or media specialist and have him or her locate a large selection of appropriate books from which students can choose. Another possibility is to compile a list of resources available in the school library, or to provide your students with the call numbers of sections of the library containing related literature. Be sure to include technology resources.

During this activity, have students each begin a portfolio of materials about sailing. Have them start a journal in which they list and write about all related books they read. Then ask them to make journal entries each day at the conclusion of each activity. Students should collect all unit materials in the portfolio.

Evaluation: based on observation of students' use of books and on examination of portfolio and journal entries

ACTIVITY THREE

Discussion

Objective: to carry on a discussion of individual reading and research completed in Activity Two, and to begin planning subsequent activities

Materials: paper and drawing instruments

poems or songs about sailing as desired

Procedure: Lead your students in a discussion about sailboats based on what they have discovered from both first-hand experience and from their readings. Through this discussion, lead students to consider the possibilities of going sailing, constructing model sailboats, and holding a model-sailboat regatta. Have each child draw a picture showing what his or her sailboat for the regatta will look like. This might be an appropriate time to introduce a poem or song about sailing.

Evaluation: participation in class discussion including the readings from Activity Two, completion of drawing

ACTIVITY FOUR

Testing Hull Designs

Objective: to view and test various hull (body of boat) designs, to record the results of these tests, and to learn about the factors influencing these test results

Materials: precut soft-wood blocks

string

spring scale

tank table (see Figure 2.3)

Procedure: Supply your class with the materials listed above. Set up a test tank using a sturdy table, 2×6 lumber, and polyethelene sheeting.

Display and describe the three hull shapes illustrated in Figure 2.3. Attach string to each shape. Have children test the several hull designs by pulling the blocks through the tank and recording the spring-scale reading.

FIGURE 2.3
Sailboat and tank table

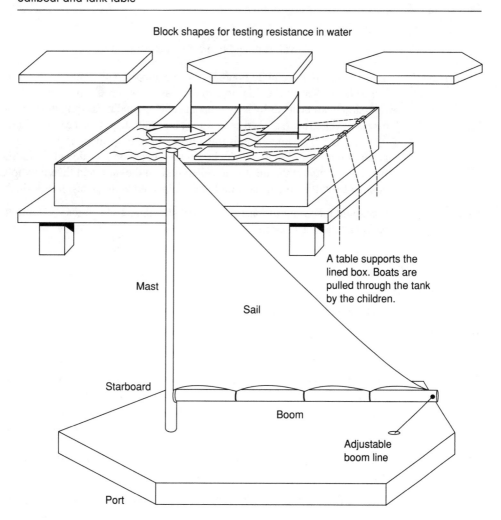

Finally, hold a short discussion about and record the results of the boat tests on the chalk-board. The results probably will not show any clear pattern because the children will have pulled the boats through the water at different speeds. Lead the discussion towards the consideration of how the activity can be redesigned so that the results of different groups using the same blocks will be similar. Make sure the children understand that the boat's resistance depends on its speed and the force applied in pulling. Point out that they must pull the boats at the same speed and measure the force, or pull with the same force and measure the speed.

Evaluation: successful completion and recording of test results, participation in discussions

ACTIVITY FIVE

Measuring Speed

Objective: to learn how to measure speed and test for relative resistance, and to mount a mast and attach a sail and boom to a model boat

Materials: tank table (see Activity Four)

pendulum

wooden block, dowel, sail, and boom for each student

Procedure: The tank set up for Activity Four should be equipped with thread spools so that applied force can be held constant. Demonstrate to the class how speed can be measured in two ways: by comparing two boats or by setting up a pendulum and measuring the time duration of a boat over a measured course. Then demonstrate how hull shapes can be tested for relative resistance.

When the class understands this information, have them collect data using the pulley-pendulum system. Supply each child with a piece of 1/4" dowel stick. Show the children first how to mount the mast in a drilled hole in the hull, and then how to attach a sail and boom. Carefully store these simple boats, labeled with names, for use in the next activity.

Evaluation: successful mounting of mast to hull and attachment of sail and boom to the mast, participation in class discussion

ACTIVITY SIX

Complete Boats

Objective: to complete and test individual sailboats

Materials: all of those listed for Activities Four and Five

two electric fans

Procedure: This activity should include time for the children to work individually on their sailboats. You should set up two electric fans by the tank so that when the boats are completed, their sails can be tested. Problems that arise should be noted and discussed.

While this seems like a simple activity, it will probably require a full class period. You should be free to move throughout your class, giving individual help and advice as it is needed. It is helpful to have several good resource books for students to refer to while they are waiting for your personal attention.

Evaluation: successful completion of individual sailboats, testing of those boats through the use of the fans

ACTIVITY SEVEN

Boat Modifications

Objective: to modify boats as needed, to plan the regatta

Materials: no new materials are required, but material to detail the boats such as paint and sandpaper could be provided

Procedure: Children should be given time to modify and test their sailboats based on the results of Activity Six. Discuss with the children plans for holding a regatta on an outdoor lake or pond or an indoor pool. Committees should be set up to work out details for the regatta, including activities, races, rules, and allowable boat modifications (e.g., smooth hulls, paint, and maximum sail area).

Your role during this activity again will be to move freely around the classroom, answering questions as they come up, guiding children to the materials needed, and giving advice about modifications desired or required for a successful sailboat. Your aid will also be needed by the committees responsible for setting up the regatta and related events.

Evaluation: successful completion of all boat modifications, completion of plans for the regatta

ACTIVITY EIGHT

Regatta and Display of Boats

Objective: to provide a recreational chance for students to sail their boats and compete in one or more races with them

Materials: awards as desired (e.g., ribbons or certificates)

Procedure: The final activity in this unit is to stage a regatta using the model boats created in class. This should be carried out based on the committee work done within the student groups.

Think about awarding all boats a commemorative sail emblem, or developing ribbons for many categories so that each boat will have a display ribbon. Categories might be: run winners, race winners, hull design, art work, craftsmanship, and first boat to tip.

Keep in mind that the main objective of this final activity is a recreational one. Make sure that each child in your class enjoys the regatta and finishes the unit feeling good about his or her participation in it.

Evaluation: participation in the regatta

ADDITIONAL ACTIVITIES

Extension or Evaluation

1. A student in your class may know an ardent sailor who could serve as a resource person. There also may be nautical exhibits, marine museums, or harbor facilities in your area that the class could visit. A local ROTC Naval officer could be invited to discuss the history of naval craft and answer children's questions. These are all examples of how the small-scale activities of this unit can be expanded to experiences involving full-sized sailboats.

2. Point out to your students that locating a position on land is not difficult. Street names, addresses, and road numbers define points where specific buildings, lots, and farms are located. Explain that locating a position on water, especially when out of sight of land,

FIGURE 2.4
Using triangulation techniques for finding locations

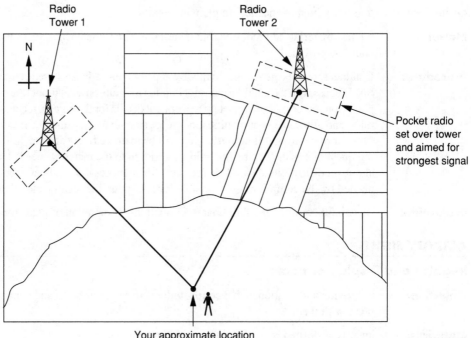

is a bit more difficult. Provide the class with information about the history and development of sea navigation, focusing specifically on latitude and longitude and devices used to measure them.

3. Today, ship captains use several electronic locating devices. Have your students find out about LORAN (**L**ong **R**ange **N**avigation), radio compasses, and satellites that send signals to help ships instantly locate their position. As illustrated in Figure 2.4, students can locate their position on a state map if they know the location of two radio-station transmitting towers. Using the map, circle two radio-tower locations. Lay the map flat and turn it so that north on the map points north. Set a small transistor radio on the map and tune in a station. Rotate the radio, and when the signal is strongest, draw a line from the center of the radio across the map in line with the radio. Repeat this for the second radio station. Extend the two lines until they cross. The intersection should be at, or very close to, the point where you are located.

4. Have students make a display of sailboats or pictures of sailboats.

5. Have students write a song about sailing.

6. Invite a sailing enthusiast to speak to the class about his or her sailboat. Plan interview questions in advance.

7. Have students investigate wind surfing.

8. Ask students to locate places where sailing is possible in your community. Have them make a class map of the locations.

FIGURE 2.5
Curriculum areas planning chart: Sailboats

Curriculum Areas:	1	2	3	4	5	6	7	8	*
Whole Language	•	•	•	•	•	•	•	•	•
Mathematics		•	•	•	•	•	•		•
Science	•	•	•	•	•	•	•		•
Social Studies	•	•	•			•	•		•
Physical Education			•					•	
Arts			•	•	•	•	•		•
Music			•						•

Column header group: Activity Number

9. Have children write stories or poems about sailing and include illustrations.

10. Collect books about sailing for your classroom. These might include the following:

    Boats by Ken Robbins. Scholastic, 1989.
    Amazing Boats by Margarette Lincoln. Alfred Knopf, 1992.
    Boats and Boating by Alistair Hamilton MacLaren. Bookright Press, 1992.
    Ships and Boats by Angela Royston. Aladdin Books, 1992.
    This Is Sailing by Richard Creagh-Osborne and Peter A.G. Milne. W.W. Norton, 1978.

    You also might check with your school librarian for available resources.

11. Have interested students check for Internet connections or videotapes to share with the class.

Teacher Resources See Appendix B for resources and addresses.

Curricular Areas. Once you have planned your lessons, it is important to carefully examine them to be sure you really have included more than one curricular area. A curriculum areas chart such as the one shown in Figure 2.5 can help you with this. Sometimes there will be overlap in one lesson. For example, a certain measurement activity might integrate mathematics, science, and social studies. A blank curriculum areas chart is provided in Appendix A-VI for your future use.

Learning Styles. Your lessons also need to be carefully examined to make sure that they include activities to meet the varied learning styles in your classroom. Table 2.1 indicates activities that are suitable for the various learning styles. Again, there might be overlap in one lesson. It is important to remember that not all learning styles or curricular areas need to be covered in any one unit. However, those that are not included in the unit you currently

TABLE 2.1
Activities for various learning styles

Learning Styles	Activity
Linguistic	write
	read
	tell stories
Logical/	do experiments
Mathematical	ask questions
	figure things out
	compute
	examine patterns
Spatial	draw
	build
	watch movies, tapes
	use machines
	check software or Internet
Musical	sing
	listen to music
	use instruments
Kinesthetic	move around
	talk
	use body language
Intrapersonal	work alone
	pursue own ideas
Interpersonal	work in groups
	have lots of friends
	talk to others

FIGURE 2.6
Learning styles planning chart: Sailboats

Learning Styles:	Activity Number								
	1	2	3	4	5	6	7	8	*
Linguistic	•	•	•	•	•	•	•	•	•
Logical/Mathematical	•	•	•	•	•	•	•	•	•
Visual	•	•	•	•	•	•	•		•
Musical			•						•
Kinesthetic			•	•	•	•		•	•
Intrapersonal		•	•			•	•		•
Interpersonal	•		•	•	•		•	•	•

are planning should be considered for the next unit. This should apply to all of the areas you are checking as you plan. Figure 2.6 illustrates how you can use a learning styles chart to ensure that the activities you plan meet the needs of students with various learning styles. A blank learning styles chart is provided in Appendix A-VII.

Questioning. Another important area to consider during planning is questioning. A firm foundation first must be established at students' knowledge and comprehension levels. Once this is accomplished, you can focus questions at the application, analysis, synthesis, and evaluation levels. The levels of Bloom's *Taxonomy of Educational Objectives* can help you decide on the types of questions as well as the activities that are appropriate for your class. Table 2.2 indicates the types of questions that are appropriate for students' levels of understanding. Figure 2.7 indicates the levels of questions posed in each of the activities developed for the sailboat unit. A blank levels of questioning chart is provided for your future use in Appendix A-VIII.

Levels of Taxonomy	Verbs
Knowledge	repeat
	define
	name
	list
Comprehension	restate
	identify
	discuss
	explain
Application	dramatize
	apply
	demonstrate
	illustrate
Analysis	distinguish
	examine
	compare
	debate
Synthesis	compose
	create
	propose
	design
Evaluation	judge
	evaluate
	assess
	appraise

TABLE 2.2

Classifying questions according to levels of taxonomy

FIGURE 2.7
Levels of questioning planning chart: Sailboats

Levels of Questions	Activity Number								
	1	2	3	4	5	6	7	8	*
Knowledge	•	•	•	•	•	•	•		•
Comprehension	•	•	•	•	•	•	•		•
Application				•	•	•	•		•
Analysis				•	•	•	•		•
Synthesis				•	•	•	•		•
Evaluation								•	•

Inclusion.   The final step in planning any unit is to check it for sensitivity to inclusion. Each unit should reflect multicultural awareness, be gender-fair, and be accessible to students with disabilities. An inclusion chart, shown in Figure 2.8, can help you ensure that the units you plan are fair to all your students. Another aid, an inclusion checklist, can help you assess whether you are treating all your students fairly. A blank inclusion chart is provided in Appendix A-IX and an inclusion checklist in Appendix A-X.

Evaluation

The final step in the development of a thematic unit is assessing student progress. Both formal and informal evaluation techniques should be considered, based upon your school

FIGURE 2.8
Inclusion planning chart: Sailboats

Inclusion	Activity Number								
	1	2	3	4	5	6	7	8	*
Multicultural	•	•	•				•		•
Gender-fair	•	•	•	•	•	•	•	•	•
Disabled							•	•	•

requirements and class needs. As part of the evaluation process, students should complete their KWL sheets if they are a part of your unit. Figure 2.9 shows a completed KWL sheet for the sailboat unit. A unit checklist also can be developed for evaluating students' progress throughout the unit, as shown in Figure 2.10.

FIGURE 2.9
Completion of **K**now-**W**ant to Know-**L**earned (KWL) Sheet: Sailboats

Sailboats

What I **K**now	What I **W**ant to Know	What I **L**earned
Sailing is fun.	More about the kinds of sailboats.	I would like to have a sailboat.
We have places near our school where there are sailboats being used.	How to make a sailboat.	Sailing is fun.
	How to make a sailboat go faster.	I made and raced a sailboat and it was a lot of work.
You need wind.	Who uses sailboats?	
Sailboats come in many shapes and sizes.	Have people used sailboats for a long time?	Sailboats have been used for a long time.
	How do you know where you are if you can't see land?	I found out how to make it go faster.

FIGURE 2.10
End-of-unit activity and evaluation checklist

	Sailboat Introduction	Research Center Search	Discussion	Testing Hull Designs	Measuring speed	Complete Boats	Boat Modifications	Regatta and Display of Boats		
Names	1	2	3	4	5	6	7	8	KWL	BOX
Ben	✓	✓	✓	✓	✓	✓		✓	✓	✓
Allison	✓	✓	✓	✓	✓	✓	✓	✓	✓	✓
Juan	✓	✓	✓	✓		✓	✓	✓	✓	✓
Mark	✓	✓	✓	✓	✓	✓	✓	✓	✓	✓
Li	✓	✓	✓	✓	✓	✓		✓	✓	✓
Brandon	✓	✓	✓	✓	✓	✓	✓	✓	Inc.	✓
Jason	✓	✓	✓	✓	✓	✓	✓	✓	✓	+
Rebecca	✓	✓	ab	ab	✓	✓	✓	✓	✓	✓
Sally	✓	✓	✓						✓	Inc.

A final project often is used for student evaluation. For example, you can have students work individually to make a pattern box integrating what they have learned from the unit. Figure 2.11 illustrates a tagboard box pattern that was used to make a sailboat box. Each side of the box contains a sentence and a picture that explains something that has been learned about sailing or sailboats.

You may choose to use some type of formal evaluation instead of a final project. Or, you could use a checklist for evaluating group work instead of or in addition to an individual

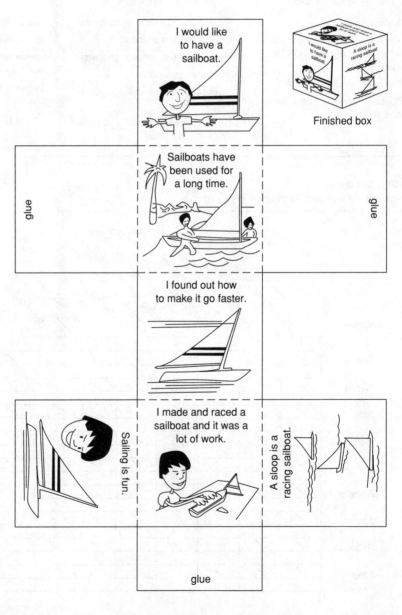

FIGURE 2.11
Unit evaluation pattern box:
Sailboats

evaluation checklist. Several types of evaluation sheets are provided for your future use in Appendices A-XI through A-XIII.

After you have tried a thematic unit approach, it is important to assess the unit. The development of thematic units, the assessment of student progress, and the measurement of effectiveness of the parts of the thematic unit are illustrated in Figure 2.12.

FIGURE 2.12
Simplified flowchart of thematic-unit development

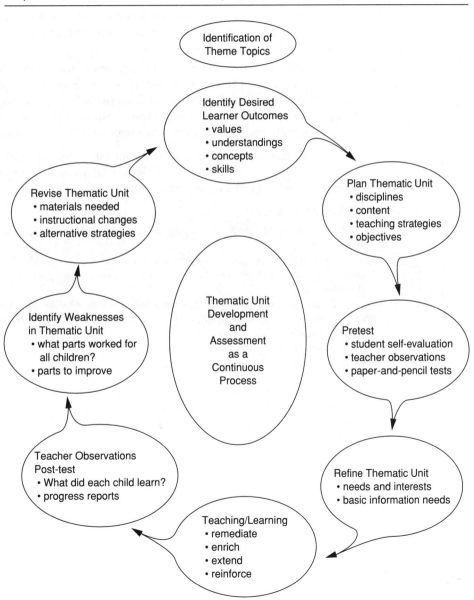

IN SUMMARY

- When you use a thematic unit as your instructional guide, you must follow a clear set of operations and procedures.

- The theme must come out of joint teacher-student planning.

- Guidance, direction, and suggestions come from the teacher.

- The teacher's role shifts from dispenser of information to facilitator of learning.

- The teacher must identify appropriate and desired learning outcomes and use them to assess children's progress.

- The teacher must provide many opportunities for children to succeed, to report, and to display work, while at the same time setting and maintaining quality standards so that children take pride in their accomplishments.

- Lastly, you must be patient and have faith. Anyone can teach a child to recite a nursery rhyme. A master teacher helps children build concepts, learn to solve problems, generate new ideas, and create new knowledge. Unfortunately, if one is to judge from tests, we often place more credence in the teacher's worth when children get high scores on standardized tests rather than when they become creative problem solvers and idea generators.

Now that you have completed your thematic unit on sailboats, you are ready to try some others. In Chapter 3 we provide a variety of additional units for you to examine. Some additional resources related to planning interdisciplinary units follow.

Additional Resources

Allen, D., & Piersma, M. (1995). *Developing thematic units: Process and product*. Albany, NY: Delmar.

Beane, J. (Ed.). (1995). *Toward a coherent curriculum*. Alexandria, VA: ASCD.

Carroll, J., & Kear, D. (1993). *A multicultural guide to thematic units for young children*. Carthage, IL: Good Apple.

Devers, W., & Cipielewski, J. (1993). *Every teacher's thematic booklist*. New York: Scholastic.

Ellis, A. (1995). *Teaching and learning elementary social studies* (5th Ed.). Needham Heights, MA: Allyn & Bacon.

Ellison, L. (1993). *Seeing with magic glasses*. Arlington, VA: Great Ocean.

Post, T. (1992). *Teaching mathematics in grades K–8: Research-based methods*. Needham Heights, MA: Allyn & Bacon.

Sadowski, M. (1995, September/October). Moving beyond traditional subjects requires teachers to abandon their "Comfort Zones." *The Harvard Educational Letter*, XI(5).

Wakefield, A. (1993, Winter). Developmentally appropriate practice: Figuring things out. *The Educational Forum*, 57(2), 134–45.

CHAPTER 3

What?
A Sampler of Thematic Units

- Transportation: Flight
- Communication: Newspapers
- Consumerism
- Time
- Change: Growing and Using Plants
- Environments
- Energy
- Inventions
- Mnemonics
- Patterns

By now, you have a basic understanding of what we mean by interdisciplinary education. You have seen how this style of teaching overcomes the artificial barriers between subject areas imposed by a traditional school curriculum, and how a connectedness can be fostered in children's awareness and understanding of their world by integrating these subject areas.

You also have learned strategies for implementing interdisciplinary units, from the planning stage through the display and evaluation of student products. More specifically, techniques have been presented for unit theme identification and development, classroom organization, questioning techniques, student expectations, and assessment and evaluation.

At this point, your head may be filled with ideas, both those that you have read and the countless others that undoubtedly popped into your mind as you considered the contents of this book. At the same time, many questions may be clouding a clear understanding of how specifically to plan and implement your own thematic units.

Each of the units in this chapter opens with a webbing diagram showing some of the general areas and specific topics and activities that can be pursued as part of the unit. This is followed by an introduction to the unit, unit objectives, and suggested appropriate grade levels. All units then go on to describe a number of activities, each containing objectives and materials lists, teaching procedures, brief evaluations, and additional activities and related resources as appropriate.

You will note, in glancing through the units that follow, that some contain pages intended for duplication. Such pages are designated within the activity plans, and are separated from the teacher's directions for easy reproduction. These pages can also be modified to better fit the skills and interests of your class. What we have given you here are examples of what can be, or has been, done with students.

It is important once again to note that good themes can be adapted for use with any age group. The classroom teacher knows best the ways in which each group of children, even at the same grade level, differ in interests, skills, and abilities. You are urged to examine these units as jumping-off points for your own curriculum development. It is our hope that the ideas and materials presented in the following units will stimulate you to develop and implement some integrated units in your classroom. We think you and your students will be pleased with the results.

THEME INTRODUCTION

This unit examines flight in general and kites as a specific mechanism of flight. Table 3.1 provides a brief overview, by curricular area, of some activities that can be pursued during this unit. Some of these are intended to be carried out with the whole class as part of your instruction concerning basic principles of flight.

Materials and resources required for this unit are easily obtainable and inexpensive. Those materials that will be used extensively include paper, cardboard, wire, sticks, and cloth. Guest speakers and field trips can be an important part of the classroom activities, but videotapes and filmstrips can be substituted. You might also be lucky enough to find TV documentaries on the air that can provide a kind of out-of-the-classroom experience. Other supplementary materials should be readily available through various local and school libraries.

TRANSPORTATION: *Flight*

Flight: Birds, airports, people, careers, kites, and flying machines all play an important role in this theme, which is rich in the diversity of possible extensions. An example of a student performance contract is included in this unit.

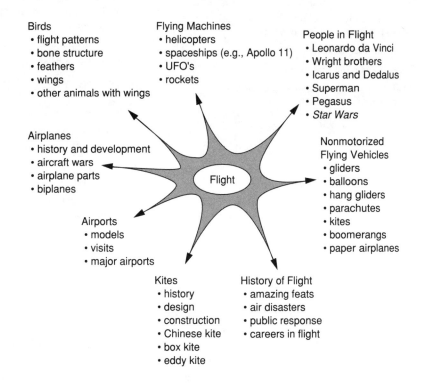

Birds
- flight patterns
- bone structure
- feathers
- wings
- other animals with wings

Flying Machines
- helicopters
- spaceships (e.g., Apollo 11)
- UFO's
- rockets

People in Flight
- Leonardo da Vinci
- Wright brothers
- Icarus and Dedalus
- Superman
- Pegasus
- *Star Wars*

Airplanes
- history and development
- aircraft wars
- airplane parts
- biplanes

Flight

Nonmotorized
Flying Vehicles
- gliders
- balloons
- hang gliders
- parachutes
- kites
- boomerangs
- paper airplanes

Airports
- models
- visits
- major airports

Kites
- history
- design
- construction
- Chinese kite
- box kite
- eddy kite

History of Flight
- amazing feats
- air disasters
- public response
- careers in flight

TABLE 3.1

Suggested activities by discipline

Literature and Language Arts

1. Read *The 21 Balloons* by William Père BuBois.
2. Fly a helium balloon. Send a message or self-addressed postcard.
3. Read flight-related poetry.
4. Read "A Bridle for Pegasus" by K. Shippen, out loud.
5. Write a description of an aerial view.
6. See Walt Disney's *Man in Flight*.
7. Read about famous flight contributors such as Lindbergh, Earhart, and Wright.
8. Write flight-related short stories.

Music and Drama

1. Sing "Up, Up and Away," "Fly Me To the Moon," and "Leaving On a Jet Plane."
2. Put on a dramatic skit of the life of a famous flight person. Videotape the skits to share with another class.

Math

1. Measure the distance of a flight with paper planes by calculating time and distance.
2. Figure the cost of airline tickets.
3. Design flight plans and routes.
4. Build models of famous planes and airports using ratio and proportion.

Field Trips and Guest

1. Visit an airport.
2. Invite a pilot to speak.
3. Invite a hang gliding expert to speak.
4. Visit a science museum.

Art

1. Display the best plane design.
2. Build and design kites.
3. Display research information with posters.
4. Draw a map from an aerial photograph.

Social Studies

1. Learn the history of flight. See *Man in Flight*.
2. Research famous people in the field of flight.
3. Study countries producing contributions to flight.
4. Study how aircraft changed wars and developed military warfare.
5. Study how aircraft changed people, politics, etc.
6. Research how airports are organized and built.
7. Explore careers related to flight, ornithology, and engineering.
8. Write to NASA about its history and future work.
9. Check your media center for any tapes or software related to flight. Prepare to share them with the class.

Science

1. Develop a basic understanding of the principles of flight by using paper airplanes in simple experiments.
2. Name the parts of a plane.
3. Name the parts of a rocket.
4. Compare the parts of a bird to the parts of a plane.
5. Build kites.
6. Complete the science contract.
7. Study flying machines—both current and early.
8. Study the parts of an insect and how flight is a part of its lifestyle.
9. Research rockets, satellites, and space exploration.

Activity One focuses on an individual Flight Contract, which you may wish to reproduce for use in your classroom. The activities included in the Flight Contract are intended for the most part to be completed by students individually. You should find the contract system to be helpful in providing some basic structure for student use of class time, setting standards for acceptable work, and evaluating performance. At the same time, however, it allows for flexibility and tends to encourage the production of high-quality work because of the high degree of individualization provided.

Unit Objectives. Students will:

1. learn some basic principles of flight.
2. complete at least one project outlined in the Flight Contract.
3. gain basic information about air movement and pressure.
4. increase their knowledge of the history and use of kites.
5. gain skills relative to independent goal setting and work completion.

Appropriate Grade Levels. Elementary and Middle School

Vocabulary.

> flight
>
> hull
>
> riggings
>
> rocketry
>
> astronauts
>
> lift
>
> drag
>
> attack angle
>
> air pressure
>
> glider

Note to Teacher: See Appendix A for planning sheets.

ACTIVITY ONE:

Flight Contract

Objective: to use the contract method to explore flight

Materials: general resource materials about flight

reproduced Activity Sheet 1: Contract for Flight

Procedure: After you introduce the topic of flight and the contract sheet, students should work alone, in pairs, or in small groups to complete the selected elements of the contract. The amount of time needed will depend upon the grade level of the students, the learning styles of the students, and the stucture of the school day.

Evaluation: successful completion of the contract

Activity Sheet 1

CONTRACT FOR FLIGHT

NAME _____

You will have class time to work on this contract from _____ to _____ (approximately $2\frac{1}{2}$ weeks). Reporting time will be every Friday.

Minimum Requirements

1. Know the basic principles of flight we work on together in class

2. Be able to pass the test on flight

3. Complete one of the following projects

Above-Average Work: 1 & 2 above plus

■ Complete two of the following activities

Top-Quality Work: 1 & 2 above plus

■ Complete three of the following activities

Projects

1. Read about the flight of the Double Eagle II balloon. Write a one- page report summarizing its flight and problems. Draw a map of where it was launched and where it landed. (See *National Geographic* magazine.)

2. Research how the inventions of the airplane affected wars, particularly World War I. A starting point might be to find out something about Count Zeppelin and his invention and how it was used in the war. Other pilots to research include Anthony Fokker or flying ace Oswald Boelcke. Two pages.

3. Do a paper on the flying ace of World War I: Baron von Richthofen, the "Red Baron." Report on his role in World War I. Maps or drawings can be included.

4. Research planes of World War II. Present pictures or drawings of each with their names. This can be done on a poster.

5. Research the life of Orville and Wilbur Wright. Two pages. Include information about where and when they lived and worked, and the problems they overcame in order to build the first successful plane. Build a model of their first plane.

6. Make a booklet of early flying machines or inventions. Include at least five. Explain when they were invented, by whom, and where. Draw a good picture of each. Examples include designs of Montgolfier, da Vinci, Lillienthal, and Cayley.

7. Make a study of birds' anatomy (body structure) and make drawings showing the parts of birds, particularly the wings. Explain in your report how a bird's design is similar to an airplane's and also how birds control their flight pattern. Gather feathers of different birds.

8. Find out the history of the parachute. In a one- to two-page report, tell who invented it, when, and how it was perfected. Explain how it works today. Build a simplified model to explain what you learned and demonstrate this in class.

9. Make a poster or bulletin board of how aircraft have changed and developed in recent years. Include pictures or drawings of each type of aircraft and a paragraph about each.

10. Research the history of gliders. Who invented and perfected the first successful gliders? Build a cardboard glider with essential parts.

11. Learn more about how airports are designed. Write to airport managers and airport designers to obtain information and report your findings. One page. Build a model of an airport.

12. Read the book *Five Weeks in a Balloon* by Jules Verne. Report to the class about it. Use a visual aid such as a poster or diorama as part of your report. Discuss this with your teacher.

13. Write about the history of ballooning—both hot-air and gas. Include the inventors and be able to explain how balloons work. Design a hot-air balloon of your own on a poster and label the parts, or build a hot-air balloon and attempt to fly it.

14. Make a large time line, to be put up in the classroom, of the most significant events in the history of flight since the time the Montgolfiers invented the hot-air balloon.

15. Research the history of rocketry beginning in America with Robert Goddard. Explain in your report how rockets work and include a diagram with the parts labeled. You can demonstrate simple experiments or build a model. (There are kits for this but they cost money.)

16. Research the history of helicopters and write a report. Build a simple model to demonstrate (not paper).

17. Research the space race between the United States and the former Soviet Union. Include information about *Sputnik I* and *II*. Discuss United States achievements in space in the early 1960s.

18. Report about the *Apollo II* landing on the moon: who the astronauts were and how they accomplished their mission. Interview three people who watched it on TV and write about their reactions at the time. Or make a poster or bulletin board about how people felt about the space race.

19. Write a complete biography of Charles Lindbergh or Amelia Earhart. Be sure to explain their greatest feats in flight history.

20. Research and collect songs that have to do with flying. Get the lyrics, titles, copyrights, and recordings if the library has any. Perform one for the class.

21. Conduct an interview with a pilot, flight attendant, or any other person whose career is associated with flight. Report to the class.

22. Check the Internet, software, or videos for material about flight to share with your class. Present at least a 10-minute report sharing what you discover.

23. If there is another project you are interested in, you may discuss it with your teacher.

I will commit myself to doing the level of work checked.

_____ Minimum _____ Above Average _____ Top Quality

Date _____ Signature _____

ACTIVITY TWO:

Kites

Objective: to introduce kites and conduct a pretest

Materials: books, films, and/or pictures about kites

chalkboard and chalk

reproduced KWL sheet (Appendix A-II) with *Kites* as heading

Procedure: Ask each student to list in the *K* column of the KWL sheet some of the things they know about kites, including an explanation of why they think kites fly. Then have them complete the *W* column to identify what they want to know. Save these sheets to measure individual growth at the end of the unit. You also can use the information on students' KWL sheets to develop the rest of this unit. Next, through discussion, a film, or pictures, present the following information to the class.

> *Kites have been around for many hundreds of years. They were used by the Chinese to communicate long before telephone or mail service was available. Instead of passing out a picture, a proud father flew a kite high into the air so that all the neighbors for miles around would know that the baby had arrived. Kites have even served the military. Giant box kites that would carry a person as a passenger were flown high above the enemy lines in World War I. Benjamin Franklin is reported to have used a kite to investigate static electricity in low storm clouds.*

Show your students pictures of a variety of kites, both simple and complex. Inform them that a simple cross kite can be built in an hour, while it may take a professional kite builder several days to make an elaborate flying ship-kite complete with hull, sails, and riggings.

You may also wish at this time to assign children to do some individual reading and research about kites and prepare reports on their findings. Or you may want to have children draw pictures of kites they would like to build, listing materials needed for constructing the kite.

Evaluation: completion of the *K* and *W* columns on the KWL sheet for kites, participation in other class discussions and activities

ACTIVITY THREE:

Small Forces Producing a Large Force

Objective: to learn that small forces together can produce a larger or greater force

Materials: small plastic bags (at least 20)

books

two tables

Procedure: To demonstrate that small forces acting together produce a large force, begin by having the children slip small plastic bags under books. They should then inflate the bags by blowing into them. Children will discover that they can lift heavy books by doing so.

Next, turn a small table upside down and place it on another table. Have children insert bags between the two tables all around the edges. At least 20 bags will be needed. At the signal *Go,* all the children should blow into the bags. If they don't succeed the first time in lifting the table, encourage them to try again. Then ask them whether this helps explain how large kites are able to lift people into the air.

Evaluation: participation in group activity

ACTIVITY FOUR:

Tethered Airfoils

Objective: to learn the meanings of the terms *lift, drag,* and *attack angle*

Materials: electric fan

10-by-20-cm pieces of tagboard

12-cm-long sticks

Procedure: Have the children attach approximately 10-by-20-cm pieces of tagboard to light sticks about 12 cm long. When they have finished, turn on the fan and instruct them to hold their cardboard in the stream of air coming from the fan, as shown in Figure 3.1. Through questioning, help them discover what such terms as *lift, drag,* and *attack angle* mean.

Following this activity, ask children to find pictures of birds, airplanes, gliders, frisbees, and other objects in flight. Ask them to describe how these objects fly using the new words they learned during the "tethered" aircraft (tagboard-and-stick apparatus) activity.

Evaluation: completion of tethered airfoil activity, correct application of new terms to related situations

ACTIVITY FIVE:

Egg in the Bottle

Objective: to learn about the force exerted by air as its pressure changes

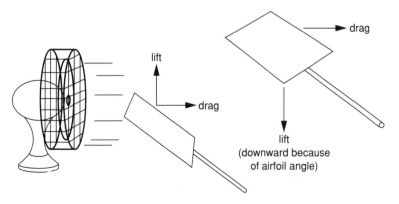

FIGURE 3.1
Tethered airfoil

Materials: small-necked bottle

peeled, hard-boiled egg

paper

matches

Note: Be sure to try this in advance.

Procedure: You will need a bottle whose neck is smooth and slightly smaller in diameter (about 5 mm) than a peeled, hard-boiled egg. Make a twist of paper and light it with a match. Drop the lighted paper into the bottle and quickly set the egg on the bottle's mouth. If everything goes according to plan, the egg will squeeze together and slide into the bottle with a loud plop. Have children try to guess why this happens. If they can't explain it, tell them that the flame heats the air, causing the air in the bottle to expand. The egg may bounce a bit as the warm air escapes. When the flame goes out, the air in the bottle cools and contracts, and the air pressure in the bottle drops. The greater outside air pressure then pushes the egg into the bottle.

You can remove the egg by inverting the bottle and blowing air past the egg. If you force enough air into the bottle, its pressure will push the egg back out. Be very careful not to swallow the egg as it comes out of the bottle.

Children can feel the pressure change in the bottle by placing a hand, which has been moistened to ensure a good seal, over the bottle just as the scrap of burning paper is dropped into the bottle. The bottle will "magically" stick to their hands! Discuss how "invisible" air can exert considerable force as its pressure changes.

Evaluation: participation in class activities

ACTIVITY SIX:

The Bernoulli Effect

Objective: to learn about the pressure exerted by air in motion (the Bernoulli effect)

Materials: Ping-Pong balls (two or more)

string

plastic straws

vacuum cleaner

beach ball or other lightweight ball

thread spools

tagboard discs

straight pins

Note: Try these in advance.

Procedure: According to Daniel Bernoulli, the pressure of air in motion is less than the pressure of motionless air. You can set up several interesting demonstrations to prove this. These demonstrations are illustrated in Figure 3.2. The first one requires two Ping-Pong balls, some string, and a plastic straw. Fasten the balls to a piece of string about 75 cm in length,

FIGURE 3.2
Bernoulli effect activities

Demonstration 1   Demonstration 2   Demonstration 3

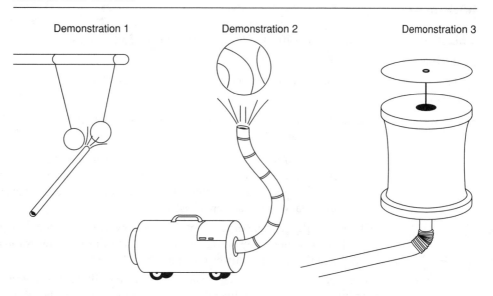

with one ball at each end. Hang the string over a support so that the balls hang loosely about one cm apart. Blow air between the Ping-Pong balls using the straw to produce a strong jet. The balls will move together. Although these and other experiment directions are written as if you are performing for your children to watch, you may wish to involve them more directly in carrying out the steps involved.

A second demonstration is one often used in stores to attract customers' attention to vacuum cleaner displays. Using a vacuum cleaner and a hose attachment, blow a jet of air upward. Toss a light ball into the stream of air. The ball will bob from one side of the stream to the other but will not leave the stream and will appear to be suspended in midair.

A third demonstration involves the use of a thread spool and a disc that has been cut from tagboard and pierced through the center with a common pin. Have several students each fasten a plastic hose into the hole of a spool. Then have them each insert a pin with a disc of tagboard on it into the opposite end of the spool. Have them try to blow the disc off the spool. If someone keeps a continuous stream of air flowing through the spool, the cardboard cannot be blown off even if the spool is turned over and the cardboard hangs without apparent support.

After these demonstrations are completed, discuss the fact that, in each case, the quickly moving air has a lower pressure than the surrounding air. The air surrounding the Ping-Pong balls exerted greater pressure, pushing them together. The air outside of the air jet from the vacuum cleaner pushed the ball back into the lower-pressure area in the stream. The air pressure on the side of the tagboard away from the spool was greater than the quickly moving air between the spool and the tagboard. Extend this by explaining that when a curved surface is moved through the air or forced into moving air, the air moves faster over the curved side than over the flat side. Thus, the air on the flat underside of a curved wing or curved kite body exerts greater pressure and lifts the wing or the kite.

Evaluation: participation in class activities, ability to explain or describe the Bernoulli effect

ACTIVITY SEVEN:

Back to Kites

Objective: to learn about the effect of lift, drag, and angle of attack on kites

Materials: electric fan

cardboard kites of three different sizes, with string and tails

sticks

Procedure: Have the children investigate the behavior of a small kite in the stream of air produced by a fan. Following are a few questions for investigation.

1. Does the area of the kite relate to lift and drag? To answer this, have your students cut three different-sized kites from cardboard and fasten each to a stick. These then can be held in the air stream, one at a time. The distance from the fan and the angle of each kite to the air stream should be kept constant.

2. If you change the angle of attack of the kite, how do lift and drag change? The children will have to devise a way of rotating the kite in the air stream, measuring its attack angle and measuring (or carefully estimating) lift and drag.

3. Does the angle of attack relate to how high the kite will fly? Students will have to devise a way to measure the height of the kite. In each test, the string length should be held constant, with only the bridle connections being changed.

4. Does the length of the tail and the attack angle relate to the stability of the kite? Make clear to your students that in the case of two-variable problems, only one variable at a time should be changed. By the time this investigation is completed, your students should have learned that a stable kite flies in a vertical position with little or no bobbing and swooping.

Evaluation: participation in group activities, understanding of modifications needed to make kites fly

ACTIVITY EIGHT:

Kite Building

Objective: to select a kite design and construct a kite

Materials: kite-building materials (paper, sticks, string, etc., with specifics dependent on the type of kites to be built)

kite plans, printed separately or in books

Note: This activity may take several days to complete.

Procedure: Your students by now have learned about some scientific principles that relate to flight. Now it is time for them to put these findings into practice.

Distribute plans for several kites, or allow time for students to select plans from printed sheets or resource books. Provide the children with rulers and meter sticks. Supply sheets of newsprint or wrapping paper. Have children enlarge the plans for the kite of their choice to full scale. Have them check their materials list against their plans.

Once students are ready to begin making their kites, you should hold short skill sessions as needed, showing all children or small groups of children how to carry out some of the construction operations (stick cutting and fastening, paper covering, coloring, decorating, attachment of bridle, and construction and attachment of tails). You also will need to give assistance to individuals throughout the building of the kites.

Evaluation: kite construction begun from selected kite plans or patterns

ACTIVITY NINE:

Kite Testing

Objective: to test the ability of the kites to fly and make any final adjustments needed

Materials: none needed, unless extensive modifications are required

Procedure: Each child's kite should now be nearly or fully completed and ready for a preliminary flight. Have students take their kites onto the playground and fly them. Observe carefully and keep records of each kite's performance. Have students consider the following questions.

1. Did my kite rise? How fast? How high?
2. Was it stable?
3. What problems, if any, were encountered?
4. What could be done to improve my kite's flight?

Once you're back in your classroom, hold small-group problem-solving sessions. These should include reviews of concepts that the children may need to keep in mind in order to solve their kite problems. These sessions may be devoted to problems such as wind force, kite lift, bridle attachment, balance, and stability. Provide time in which the children can make whatever modifications they determine are necessary.

Evaluation: correct identification of any flight problems and completion of necessary modifications

ACTIVITY TEN:

Kite Flying Day

Objective: to fly individual kites and evaluate the flights of all kites made

Materials: none needed

Procedure: This is the big day! By now, at least the major bugs should have been worked out, and all kites should be decorated and ready to go. Before the event, you may wish to make and display posters in your school describing the event and inviting others in the school to attend. Since weather is important, your plans should include several alternate dates.

On kite day, begin by having the children fly all of the kites together, making individual adjustments as needed. When all of the problems have been solved, have students fly kites one at a time. Discuss how each kite behaves and how it could be improved. When all the children have had a turn, you can finish by again having them fly all kites at once. You may wish to end the unit by having students draw pictures or write stories about their kite flying and display the kites in the school where everyone can enjoy them. One or more photos of the kites would also be a nice record of the event. However, it is doubtful that *any* record will be needed to help your students remember the culmination of the unit!

Evaluation: flight of all kites

UNIT EVALUATION: KITE BOOK

Objective: to explain key information learned about flight

Materials: pattern (see Figure 3.3)   string
                   construction paper   glue
                   crayons and markers

Procedure: Have students work in pairs to make a multiflap book that explains and illustrates six key points they have learned about flight. Have each pair make from construction paper a large pattern like the one shown in Figure 3.3. Then have them write a sentence on each square and make a picture on each flap. Next, they will cut out the squares on the dotted lines and then cut out the flaps and glue the squares behind the matching numbered flaps. Have the students finish by decorating the kites and adding a tail to each one.

ADDITIONAL ACTIVITIES:

Extension and Evaluation

1. Help your students investigate aerial photography. Check the library or resource center for any audio-visual materials, software, or Internet connections related to this topic.

2. Contact a sports store to see if you can locate a person who knows about hang gliding. Perhaps that person would be willing to talk to the class and be interviewed, or give a demonstration.

3. If there is a kite store in your neighborhood or city, you could contact the owner to see whether you could take the class to the shop or whether he or she could bring some kites to your class. Asian stores or museum shops with kites for sale or on display might also be located nearby.

4. Have students investigate the Japanese Boys' Festival on May 5 and make carp kites.

5. Have students write poems or songs about flight.

6. Visit your local airport.

7. Have students read about Benjamin Franklin's kite experiment.

8. Develop a bulletin board entitled *Up and Away.*

9. Have students listen to "You Can Fly" from *Mary Poppins* or "The Kite" from *Peter Pan.*

10. Extend the unit to include land transportation.

11. Make a classroom display of books about flight for children. Your school or public library is likely to contain many resource books. See Appendix B for additional sources.

Teacher Resources

Transportation by Mel Fuller. Grand Rapids, MI: Instructional Fair, Inc., 1992.
Flight by Judy Vaden. Huntington Beach, CA: Teacher-Created Materials, 1991.
Kites and Hot Air Balloons by Janet Bruno. Cypress, CA: Creative Teaching Press, Inc., 1990.
Making Kites by David Michael. New York: Kingfisher Books, 1993.

See Appendix B for addresses.

FIGURE 3.3
Kite book

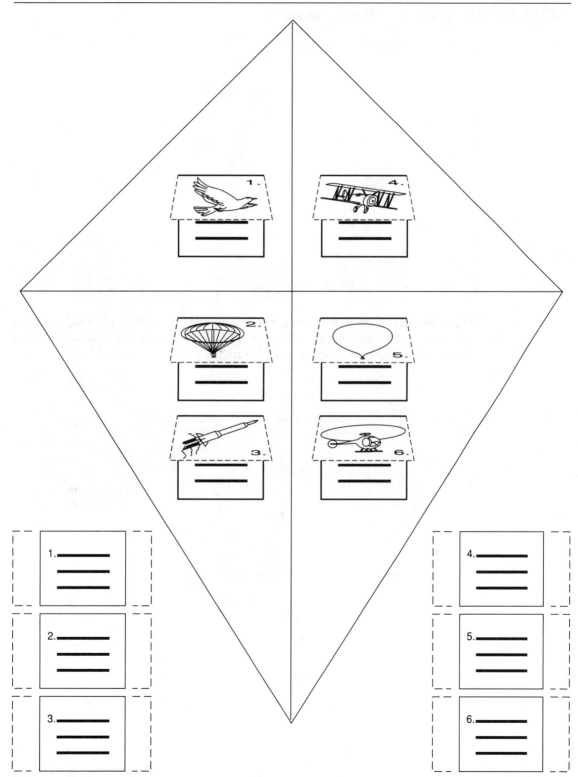

COMMUNICATION: Newspapers

Read All About It: Headlines, sports, advertisements, polls, and comic strips are investigated and discussed for an in-depth consideration of the daily newspaper. The effective design of a newspaper-related learning station is illustrated.

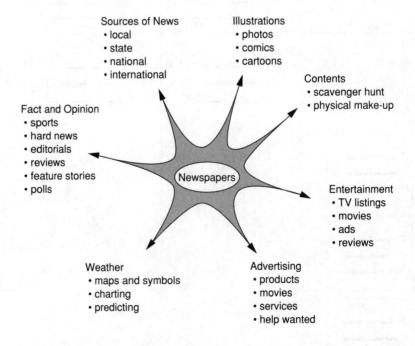

Sources of News
• local
• state
• national
• international

Illustrations
• photos
• comics
• cartoons

Contents
• scavenger hunt
• physical make-up

Fact and Opinion
• sports
• hard news
• editorials
• reviews
• feature stories
• polls

Newspapers

Entertainment
• TV listings
• movies
• ads
• reviews

Weather
• maps and symbols
• charting
• predicting

Advertising
• products
• movies
• services
• help wanted

INTRODUCTION

The daily newspaper represents a valuable source of materials and ideas for a thematic unit. On a typical day, a newspaper contains science, math, language, social studies, and other areas of the curriculum waiting to be taught. Consider for a moment the photographs, maps, stories, advertisements, graphs, and statistical information found in the newspaper on any given day. You might be surprised to learn that the average daily newspaper contains approximately 150,000 words exclusive of want ads. That is the size of a small novel. Sunday papers, of course, are much larger and more varied in their content.

Perhaps you have thought of the newspaper as something only for adults, or at most as a possible current-events source for senior high school students. There are, however, many possible educational uses of the newspaper with elementary and middle school students. In fact, the perception that the newspaper is for adults can add to the motivational aspect of learning once students find that they can achieve success using this tool.

In recent years, newspapers have lost readership. Declining circulation has been a fact of life for nearly every metropolitan daily. This has been the case for a number of reasons: rises in postage rates, increased costs of advertising, and the high cost of newsprint. A recent survey determined four major reasons that people give for not subscribing to a newspaper:

1. I don't have time to read it.
2. I can't afford it.
3. I already heard it on TV.
4. There is nothing in there that interests me.

These reasons, given by adults, are of significant interest to the teacher whose instructional objectives include basic literacy, the development of an informed citizenry, and awareness of technological, economic, and social developments. To help teachers meet the challenge of the encroachment of television and other competing factors as threats to literacy (e.g., a half-hour television news broadcast has about 6,000 words, barely the equivalent of a newspaper's headlines), most major newspapers in the United States and Canada have developed newspaper-in-education programs. You can be quite sure that the major daily in your state or province has a program. Contact your newspaper for help with ideas for using the newspaper in your classroom.

Unit Objectives. Students will:

1. be able to differentiate between fact and opinion, and learn the values of each in a newspaper.
2. be able to identify various kinds of information in newspapers and to locate them.
3. be able to locate various sections of the newspaper.
4. be able to differentiate among local, state, national, and international news.

Appropriate Grade Levels. Elementary and Middle School

Vocabulary.

fact	cutline
opinion	jumpline
editorial	flag
propaganda	banner
cut	communication

Note: See Appendix A for planning sheets.

ACTIVITY ONE:

Introduction to the Newspaper

Objective: to become familiar with the format of a newspaper, and to begin learning newspaper terminology before using the learning center.

Materials: newspapers

paper and pencils

Procedure: Write *communication* on the board. Discuss what it means. Then hand out newspapers to all students and allow them free reading time for about 10 minutes. Then ask students to go back and count how many different sections and how many stories they read. This activity allows students freedom of choice in their reading and makes them feel comfortable with the newspaper.

Spend the rest of the period taking students through the newspaper section by section. Explain the importance of each section. Show students the types of information they can find in each section. As you go through the newspaper, you may wish to identify terminology used in the newspaper world. For example: banner, a headline that extends across the newspaper; flag, the name of the paper; cut, a photo; cutline, a photo caption; and jumpline, a line indicating that the article is continued on another page. You might want the students to begin a scrapbook containing specific examples of the terminology or types of writing as you continue the discussion.

Finally, explain to students that there are many different kinds of newspapers, some of which have different functions from a metropolitan daily. Have them bring in other newspapers they might receive at their homes and share them with the rest of the class. These can be tacked up for display.

Evaluation: completion of activities, participation in discussions

ACTIVITY TWO:

Sources of Information and Fact or Opinion

Objective: to correctly identify the source of information for stories, and to identify stories, as fact or opinion

Materials: newspapers

paper and pencils

Procedure: Begin by discussing the various ways in which news reaches a newspaper office. Explain what a wire service is and how it feeds information to a newspaper. Ask students to look at the front page and see whether they can determine the source of each story. Explain the importance of the dateline in determining the location of the story. Ask them why some stories have a byline and others do not.

Help your students begin to recognize fact and opinion. Tell them (unless they can tell you) that columns and articles on the editorial and opinion pages usually contain some opinion, while news stories are supposed to be free of the writer's opinions and views. All news stories are written from the greatest objectivity that reporters can achieve, with more important stories carrying a byline. In comparison, news reviews are usually labelled as opinion or analysis. They are written by columnists or appear on the editorial page. Finally, feature stories are not hard news. They are different from straight factual reports in that they give more background information and often, opinion.

Once this information has been presented and discussed, have students select a straight news story. Ask them to list the facts in the order in which they are reported. Ask them where they think the story can be cut and still give all the pertinent facts needed. Explain the importance of concise, factual, succinct writing in reporting the news. Discuss pyramid construction and its value in editing news stories. Explain that reporters use an inverted pyramid approach to writing news stories: In an inverted pyramid, "who," "what," "where," "when," and "why" are often incorporated into the story's lead paragraph, and less-important information is included in following paragraphs.

Have students locate a straight news story and then a feature story about the same subject. Ask them to write down statements that they feel express the writers' opinions. Ask them to locate words that may color the reporting. Then ask whether they think there is a place in journalism for both kinds of news reporting. You might wish to compare an editorial and a letter to an editor on the same topic. You also can show students how cartoons are used to express opinions in the newspaper.

Finally, give students a set of facts and ask them to write a straight news story not expressing any opinion and using pyramid construction.

Evaluation: successful completion of activities assigned

ACTIVITY THREE:

The Newspaper Learning Station

Objective: to set up a learning center utilizing newspaper skills in the classroom (note that this is essentially a teacher goal, except for instructions to students concerning the use of the center)

Materials: will vary (see list in text for suggestions)

Procedure: This learning station is a self-contained activity center where one student, partners, or small groups may select independent learning activities. You can use the learning station for the activities that follow, and you also can develop many other activities for the learning station. Activities can be duplicated on oak-tag and used as activity cards or on paper for individual consumption. Each activity requires students to use the newspaper. The activities are

FIGURE 3.4
Newspaper learning station

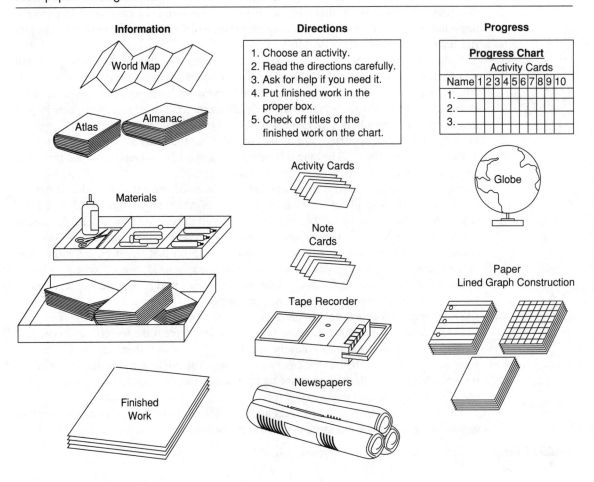

not presented in order of degree of difficulty but are categorized according to the section of the newspaper used.

As shown in Figure 3.4, the learning station design includes a bulletin board for displays and directions to the students. You might wish to identify particular areas of the display by labeling them with the words Information, Directions, and Progress, and begin to define them with brief questions and graphics. Posted directions to students might read: "Choose an activity. Read the directions carefully. Ask for help if you need it. Put finished work in the proper box. Check off the titles of the finished work on the chart. Please keep things in their proper locations for the next person."

Post the numbered list of titles of activity cards near the class list so that students can record the numerals of completed cards. You might instead choose to individualize a bit more by having a record card prepared for and completed by each student. In any case, the record kept should look something like this:

PROGRESS CHART

NAME	Activity Cards 1–10									
	1	2	3	4	5	6	7	8	9	10
1.										
2.										

Supplies and materials needed to stock the learning station might include the following:

stacks of newspapers

reference books (dictionary, atlas, and almanac)

blank outline maps

paper (lined, graph, and construction)

globe

tape recorder, blank tapes

tools (scissors, rulers, markers, and paste)

basket or bin for completed work

The learning station will help learners become familiar with the newspaper through varied activities using an interdisciplinary approach. It is designed to reinforce and extend students' academic skills and human understandings in relation to the variety of curriculum areas represented by each activity. It is hoped that as a result of these activities, students will pursue special interests of their own or those suggested under Additional Activities.

Evaluation: participation in learning station

The following activities can be conducted by the whole class or by smaller groups using the learning station set up in Activity Three.

ACTIVITY FOUR:

A Scavenger Hunt

Objective: to find and identify various sections of a newspaper

Materials: newspapers

paper and pencils

scissors

reproduced Activity Sheet 4: Scavenger Hunt

Procedure: Give students the opportunity to explore the newspaper and find and identify its many parts. You can either use the Scavenger Hunt sheet provided or choose items of interest to you and provide them to your students in a similar format.

Evaluation: successful completion of assigned items on Scavenger Hunt

Activity Sheet 4

SCAVENGER HUNT

Action   Use your newspaper to find the answers to the following questions. Find them as quickly as you can. Good luck!

1. What was the high temperature yesterday? _____

2. Give the headline of the article on the front page that you feel was most important. _____

3. Where do you find information on the number of calendar days left in this year, and the time of sunrise and sunset? _____

4. How many sections does the paper have? _____

5. On what page do you find the first classified ad? _____

6. What telephone number do you call if you want to subscribe to the paper? _____

7. Name a person written about in a feature article. _____

8. Does this issue have a correction to an earlier issue? _____

9. Who drew the cartoon on the editorial page? _____

10. Who is the managing editor of the paper? _____

11. How many letters from readers are there? _____

12. What is one subject of an advice column today? _____

13. How many couples applied for a marriage license? _____

14. How many baby girls were born? _____ Baby boys? _____

15. List one movie advertised. _____

16. What food item do you think is the best buy in a grocery ad? _____

17. Name one subject discussed in home repairs. _____

18. What was the high temperature in Boston yesterday? _____

19. What programs will be on TV at 6:30 tonight? _____

20. Name a prominent person written about in the sports section. _____

21. Look for the miscellaneous section of the classified ads and copy the items to be sold in the first garage sale you find. _____

22. Articles on the front page sometimes come from different countries or cities. Find the article that came from farthest away. Name the place. _____

23. Does your paper have any connections to the Internet? If so, what are they? _____

You can develop many variations of this activity, or use the following suggestions.

1. Have students make up individual items for another Scavenger Hunt.

2. Have students work in pairs and make up a Scavenger Hunt for one section of the newspaper.

3. Repeat the Scavenger Hunt at the end of this thematic unit.

ACTIVITY FIVE:

Kinds of News

Objective: to identify news stories as local, national, or international, and to make value judgments concerning the seriousness of the news reported

Materials: newspapers

pencils, glue, and paper

reproduced Activity Sheet 5: Local, National, and International News

Procedure: It can be important to students' understanding of the meaning and importance of news stories to be aware of the origin of that news. One part of this developing understanding is the ability to identify news as local, national, or international in scope. Have students complete the activity sheet, which is designed to increase student awareness and understanding of that distinction.

Evaluation: successful completion of the activity sheet

Activity Sheet 5

LOCAL, NATIONAL, AND INTERNATIONAL NEWS

Action   1. Skim through the news section and check the datelines to find where the news happened.

2. Using color markers, mark local news stories with the letter *L*, national stories with the letter *N*, and international stories with the letter *I*.

3. Find local news stories that tell something about the following issues:
   a. crime
   b. business or industry
   c. traffic or transportation
   d. environment
   e. housing

Write the correct letter from the list near the headline of each of the local news stories. For example, a news article about a robbery would be marked with an *a*.

More   1. Look over the national news that you marked. Decide which news article tells about something that affects the most people. Cut it out, paste it on a piece of paper, and label it *N*.

2. Look over the international news you marked. Decide which news article tells about something that affects our nation's government. Cut it out, paste it on paper, and label it *I*.

3. Pretend you are Clark Kent or Lois Lane. Which problem in the world would you work on? Why? Tell in writing or show in a cartoon or sketch.

ACTIVITY SIX:

Weather Watch

Objective:	to interpret symbols on a weather map correctly
Materials:	newspapers chart paper and calendar
	paper and pencils reproduced Weather Watch activity sheet
Procedure:	Students are probably exposed daily to weather information and maps on television. Many, however, probably could not read the weather symbols on their own, since they are in the habit of listening to the information given rather than reading it. The activity sheet will give students practice in interpreting weather maps for themselves.
Evaluation:	successful completion of Activity Sheet 6: Weather Watch

Activity Sheet 6

WEATHER WATCH

Action

1. Find the weather map in today's newspaper.
2. Study the weather symbols that mean fair, cloudy, and partly cloudy.
3. Find the symbols that tell you if there will be rain, snow, or fog in your area today and tonight.
4. Draw all the symbols you find on a piece of chart paper. Make the symbols large. Show the chart to your class and talk about what the symbols mean.
5. Each day, put one of the symbols on a classroom calendar to show the day's weather.

More

1. Work with a small group. Using the weather map in the newspaper, make up questions to ask another group. For example: "Is it raining anywhere?" or "Does the southwest part of the U.S. look as though it will get rain soon?"
2. Predict what the weather will be one week from today by thinking about what the weather has been. Write down your prediction. Next week, see if your prediction is correct.
3. Watch the evening news on TV. Do the weather reporters use the same symbols as those in the newspaper?

ACTIVITY SEVEN:

Sports Opinions

Objective:	to identify fact and opinion in sports stories and to make personal value judgments about various sports
Materials:	newspapers
	paper and pencils
	reproduced Activity Sheet 7: Sports Opinions

Procedure: The activity sheet gives your students a chance to use their interest in sports to differentiate fact from opinion and to express personal preferences. As with the preceding activity, it may be reproduced and distributed or used in any other format desired.

Evaluation: successful completion of at least the Action items

---

Activity Sheet 7
SPORTS OPINIONS

Action

1. Find a sports column. Mark the name of the sports columnist and then read the column.

2. Locate and mark three facts in the column. (A fact is something that happened and can be checked out.) Use a colored marker.

3. Locate and mark three opinions in the column. (An opinion is what someone thinks or feels about what happened.) Use a different-colored marker.

4. Decide which of the following sports you would like to be really good at:

   archery   skiing

   golf   swimming

   fishing   stock-car racing

   hockey   tennis

   Number your choices in order from one to eight. Number one would be the sport you would like to be best at and number eight the sport you are least interested in.

5. Look at your list. Did you choose team sports or individual sports as your favorites? Think about your choices, then complete the following sentence: "I'm the kind of person who _____."

More

1. Find a news story about a sport you've never tried. Write your opinion.

2. Conduct an opinion survey about wrestling on TV. What did you find out?

ACTIVITY EIGHT:

Photographs and Cartooning

Objective: to find and examine photos, cartoons, and comics in the newspaper

Materials: newspapers

paper and crayons or pencils

reproduced Activity Sheet 8: Photographs and Cartooning

Procedure: Reading for entertainment is just as important as reading for fact. How do cartoons express opinions? Are all the captions under pictures found in the paper serious? Why do photographs add to any story in the paper?

Evaluation: successful completion of activities assigned or pursued

Activity Sheet 8

PHOTOGRAPHS AND CARTOONING

Action

1. Examine the comics. Name your six favorites. Tell what each comic expresses: for example, humor, irony, philosophy, a continuing story, or a moral.

2. Clip a comic that particularly appeals to you and write your own words for it.

3. Examine the different kinds of photographs in a newspaper. Clip two photographs and write new captions for them.

   The following suggestions also can be developed for this activity.

1. Have students draw their own comics and explain the purpose of their artwork. Students alternately might work in teams on this project, combining their skills and reinforcing each other in the learning process.

2. Have students make a photograph collage expressing an attitude, one or more different kinds of emotion, different kinds of action, or different kinds of people. Allowing the students to choose their own topics or themes gives them greater freedom in the learning process. However, you may wish to narrow the topic to your own subject goals. The finished collages can be displayed around the room and will create a great deal of interest in the school.

3. Have students make a word collage. Individual collages could be made into a class book.

ACTIVITY NINE:

Comics

Objective:	to read, analyze, and create various components of newspaper comics
Materials:	newspapers
	paper and drawing or writing instruments
	reproduced Activity Sheet 9: Comics
Procedure:	Have students work in pairs to complete the activity sheet.
Evaluation:	successful completion of at least the Action items

Activity Sheet 9

COMICS

Action

1. Find a comic strip in the paper.

2. Find someone to work with.

3. List the names of as many characters as you can that appear in the comic strip.

4. Choose the two characters that interest you the most. Write words that describe these two.

5. Think of new words to describe each character that would change his or her personality (Sarge—tough, loud, shy, meek). Think of new names for the characters that would go with their new personalities.

More

1. Draw a new appearance for your characters to fit their new personalities.

2. Draw a three-box comic strip using your new characters.

3. Share your new comic strip with others. See if they find it funny.

ACTIVITY TEN:

Advertising and Its Importance

Objective: to identify and evaluate kinds of advertisements and to understand their economic importance to the publishing of newspapers as well as to consumers

Materials: newspapers

paper and pencils

reproduced Activity Sheet 10: Advertising and Its Importance

Procedure: Have students browse through the newspaper to see how many different kinds of advertisements they can find: for example, political, food, products, services, or help wanted. Explain the difference between national and local ads, what display advertising is, and why the classified section is important to consumers. Ask students why they think it is important for them to be able to read ads. Discuss the economics of publishing a newspaper and why advertising is vital to the financial position of the paper.

Evaluation: successful completion of the activity sheet

Activity Sheet 10
ADVERTISING AND ITS IMPORTANCE

Action Find four examples of the following kinds of advertisements. Divide a sheet of paper into four squares. Paste one of your advertisements in each square and label it, as shown in Figure 3.5.

1. Clip an ad showing how you can save money on something you buy.

2. Find an advertisement for something you would like to have at a price you would be willing to pay.

3. Find an ad about a service you might need.

4. Find an ad showing something the advertisers would like the public to do.

5. Find an advertisement for some place you would like to go.

FIGURE 3.5
Four types of advertisements

6. Find an ad telling of something you can do or a place you can go that won't cost you anything.

7. Find an advertisement for a job you might like.

8. Find a classified ad that is selling something you might like to have.

9. Find an ad for a contest you can enter for free.

More   1. Cut out any ads that you think are inappropriate for the newspaper to use. Explain why.

2. Write an ad of your own.

ACTIVITY ELEVEN:

Taboo for You?

Objective: to use movie titles and ads to classify, describe, and make value judgments

Materials: newspapers
paper and pencils
reproduced Activity Sheet 11: Taboo for You?

Procedure: Have students complete the activity sheet.

Evaluation: successful completion of at least the Action items

Activity Sheet 11
TABOO FOR YOU?

Action   1. Skim through the newspaper to find the pages that show lists of theaters and movies.

2. Select the page that shows a theater in your neighborhood. Count and write down the number of theaters on this page that are showing films rated *X* (adults only), *R* (restricted to 17 or over unless accompanied by an adult), *PG* (parental guidance suggested), and *G* (general audiences). Write the rating symbols and show your tally like this:

X _____   PG _____

R _____   G _____

3. Compare the tallies. Copy and complete this sentence: "Most of the theaters on this page are showing _____ movies. I _____ (can/cannot) see these films."

More   1. Look over the movie titles and descriptions. List the titles that fit at least three of the following:
a. comedy   e. animal
b. horror   f. musical
c. detective   g. cartoon
d. western

2. Write the title of a movie you really want to see. Explain why.

3. Conduct a survey to find out how people feel about film ratings that limit attendance on the basis of age.

UNIT EVALUATION: CLASS NEWSPAPER

Have students make a two-page class newspaper about what they have learned about newspapers. Use the computer to plan and organize each page. Share the newspaper with other classes and have each student take one home. This evaluation activity could be applied to any unit.

ADDITIONAL ACTIVITIES:

Extension and Evaluation

1. Help your students create their own monthly classroom newspaper. Set up a rotating staff to handle the various responsibilities related to writing and assembling a newspaper. Include all aspects of real newspapers that you feel are appropriate for a room product. Students also can be responsible for the distribution of their newspapers to parents, teachers, and students.

2. A great number and variety of items can be made from newspapers. With sufficient quantities of newspapers, students can create everything from baskets to book covers to tables to trays. Check with an art teacher for additional ideas.

3. You may wish to involve your students in a recycling drive. Most communities now make arrangements for the periodic collection of newspapers. Your students could set up a newspaper drive at school and take care of collecting, bundling, and delivering the newspapers to the recycling collection site.

4. Most large newspaper publishers have put together lesson materials for classroom use of their newspapers. Contact your local paper to see what educational services they provide.

5. Examine your local TV listings in the paper. Have students devise an opinion poll about favorite TV shows. Make a bar graph to report results.

6. Extend your focus on communication by examining other aspects of this theme, such as radio, magazines, and local topical papers.

7. Have students investigate how your paper is demonstrating a concern for issues such as conservation.

8. Have students find out how your paper meets the needs of the visually impaired.

Teacher Resources

Make Your Own Newspaper by Chris and Ray Harris. 1993.
Bob Adams, Inc., 260 Center Street
Holbrook, MA 02343. Phone: 1-800-872-5627.
USA Today

See Appendix B for additional resources and addresses.

CONSUMERISM

Consumerism: Using concepts such as supply and demand, economic stability, advertising, and product promotion, students critically examine and evaluate TV and newspaper advertisements, systematically collecting various types of data in the process.

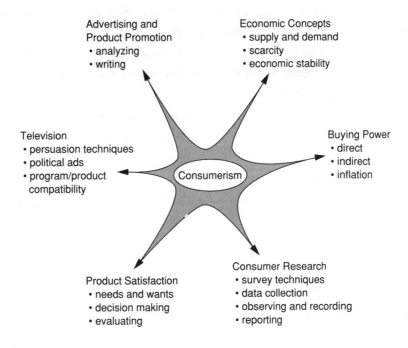

INTRODUCTION

An integrated unit on the topic of consumerism need not be a fabricated, contrived set of exercises for students. Students are themselves consumers of a wide range of products and ideas. Toys, food, clothing, CDs, sports and leisure equipment, and television programs are just a few of the things that students consume.

Of course, students are both direct and indirect consumers of goods and services. Some things they buy themselves. In many cases, goods and services are purchased for them by their parents or other adults. Like all of us, students in our society are continually bombarded with messages designed to make them want to purchase something. The various forms of coercion they are subjected to include radio and television advertising (probably the most pervasive form of advertising to this age group), messages in newspapers and magazines, and even messages printed on cereal boxes. All of these messages are then compounded by the pressure of the peer group.

What can be done from an educational point of view to make students more aware of the nature of advertising and the worth of the products that they consume? How can a study of consumerism lead to a conceptual frame of reference for students in which they begin to develop an understanding of basic economic concepts such as supply and demand, scarcity, and needs and wants? How can a consumerism unit help students develop such skills as data gathering, observing and recording, decision making, and reporting?

Questions of value, concepts, and skills are fundamental to the purpose of any interdisciplinary unit. In the consumerism activities that follow, provision is made for the development of all three of these essential concerns.

Unit Objectives. Students will:

1. be introduced to such broad concepts as supply and demand and scarcity.

2. demonstrate an awareness of the persuasive messages to which they are subjected.

3. learn to visualize their own roles as consumers.

4. make more effective decisions about the consumption of goods and services.

Appropriate Grade Levels. Elementary and Middle School

Vocabulary.

survey	supply and demand
consumerism	economic stability
advertising	promotion
advertising appeals	

Note: See Appendix A for planning sheets.

ACTIVITY ONE:

Survey Research

Objective:	to conduct a consumer research survey
Materials:	paper and pencil
	reproduced Activity Sheet 1: Survey

Procedure: Read the following story and then discuss it with your class.

> *Mary's sister Sarah, who is 7 years old, asked her mother to buy a box of cereal so that Sarah could get the free audiotape that was advertised on the back of the box. It had also been advertised several times during Saturday morning cartoon shows. Sarah's mother bought the cereal, and the family all helped Sarah eat it so she could get the tape. It was after the cereal was eaten and Sarah had the tape that the problem occurred. There was no way that Sarah could get the tape to work. Sarah was very upset and began to cry. Mary was angry too. It just didn't seem right to her that the tape was shown working fine on TV with people listening to it, but when Sarah bought the cereal, instead of laughing and enjoying it, she was crying and angry.*

After discussing the story have each student fill in the Survey form. Discuss the findings. Students also could each ask one other person to fill in the form to see whether others agreed or disagreed with the findings from your class.

Evaluation: teacher observation of successfully carried out and completed survey

---

Activity Sheet 1
SURVEY

1. Do you ever ask an adult to buy products you see advertised on TV? _____yes _____no

2. Did you ever want to buy a product to get the free bonus gift? _____yes _____no

3. Were you satisfied? _____yes _____no

4. Explain. _____

   _____

   _____

5. Do you believe that certain products you see advertised on TV make you feel happier or have more friends? _____yes _____no

6. Explain. _____

   _____

   _____

7. Did you ever feel you would be left out because you couldn't have a certain product? _____yes _____no

8. Explain. _____

   _____

   _____

9. Did you ever feel it was unfair that you couldn't buy the product you wanted? _____yes _____no

10. Explain. _____

    _____

    _____

ACTIVITY TWO:

An Inquiry into Television Advertising

Objective: to analyze the uses, appeals, and effects of television advertisements

Materials: none required

Procedure: This activity includes several parts. To carry out all of these parts will require more than one day's time. How many you choose to do and how much time you choose to allocate to each will determine the total length of time required for this activity.

Television Commercial Analysis

To help students see more clearly the "commercial" aspects of the television industry and the strong connection between individual TV programs and the products that are advertised during them, you can conduct a series of activities.

1. Make a list of every product advertised during particular popular TV programs. Then have the class discuss what the nature of these products indicates about the intended audience of the programs. What age group are they targeting? What educational level? What socioeconomic level? What values or life-style? What ethnic group?

2. Have the class participate in a matching exercise in which a number of different products and a variety of TV programs are listed, with the students determining which programs would be appropriate to carry ads for those products. Conclusions can be verified by watching the particular shows or types of shows included in the matching exercise.

3. As a homework assignment, have students conduct an ad analysis of a show of their choice, noting the products advertised and drawing conclusions about how they reveal and coincide with the intended audience for the program.

Unmarketable Programs

Have the students brainstorm the kinds of shows that are not on TV because they would appeal mainly to people who do not have the money to buy the products the sponsors want to sell, and therefore no sponsors for these shows can be found. The lack of these shows demonstrates how the consumer population determines the types of programs that are on TV.

TV Advertising Appeals Analysis

Have the students analyze the different advertising appeals used in television commercials with the objective of determining the assumed values and needs of TV viewers (e.g., the need for ego-enhancement, security, and status). Note how the programs themselves also reinforce these values and needs through the characters and situations they portray, and have the students discuss how they feel about being viewed this way (students should realize that their age group is one of the prime targets for TV ads and programs).

Political Images Through Advertising

Develop mock political campaigns with media managers and using tactics students have observed on television. Have them role-play TV spots, short documentaries, and interviews with potential voters. Encourage your students to develop a case for as well as against TV advertising in political campaigns. Have them decide whether our democratic process is helped or damaged by the increasing use of political advertising on television.

Evaluation: completion of discussions and analyses of the outlined activities (based on teacher observation)

ACTIVITY THREE:

Consumer Research on Paper Towels

Objective: to actively participate in, and complete in small groups, the researching of a particular product

Materials: five rolls of different brands of paper towels

measuring instruments, such as rulers and cups

vegetable oil

eye droppers

graph paper

Procedure: In our society, a particular product usually appears in a variety of forms under a variety of brand names. In some cases the various forms of that product are actually different with respect to quality. In other cases, the success of one brand over another may be more closely related to the amount and type of advertising used to convince consumers to buy the product.

In this activity, students will be given the opportunity to test several brands of a particular product. To get you started with product testing, we suggest you have your students test paper towels.

Bring about five rolls of different brands of paper towels to class. Remove the wrappers so students won't know what the brands are. Tell the students that their challenge is to test and rank in order the five brands from best to worst buy.

Divide the class into small groups. Explain to the groups that they need to devise and carry out several tests to determine the relative worth of the towels. Perhaps a discussion of types of appropriate tests will help students at this point. Examples of tests are dry strength, wet strength, and absorption.

Once the groups are ready to begin testing, hand out the materials needed. Tell the students they have about 45 minutes in which to complete their testing. When testing is underway, place a chart similar to the following on the board that gives information about the towels.

Color	Price	Number of Towels Per Roll	Number of Square Feet Per Roll
Blue	99¢	124	100
White	73¢	100	85
Red and White	99¢	120	85
Floral	99¢	100	100
Yellow	93¢	125	100

Some students in each group may wish to do a cost analysis, while others will proceed with the actual product testing. Encourage students to develop graphs and charts of their results.

When the testing is completed, ask each group to report its results. Not all groups will agree on the rank ordering of the paper towels. Take time to examine both the tests and the reliability of the tests used by various groups. After each group has presented its results, tell the class the name brand of each roll of towels.

Evaluation: successful completion of small-group research as presented in final written or oral format

ACTIVITY FOUR:

Write an Advertisement

Objective: to create an advertisement designed to promote a particular product

Materials: paper and drawing or writing instruments (e.g., pencils, markers, or crayons)

Procedure: Because your students have been involved in actually testing a product, they may now wish to have an opportunity to promote one. Ask students to develop an advertisement for the paper towel they felt was the best product, or ask them to develop an advertisement for an imaginary product such as a toy or movie.

Here is an example of one student's advertisement:

> BUY FLUFFO PAPER TOWELS!
> THEY'RE EVERYONE'S FRIEND!
> WITH FLUFFO, SPILLS AND MESSES
> ARE NO PROBLEM!
> BE SMART, GET FLUFFO TODAY
> AND DO YOURSELF A FAVOR!

Evaluation: successful creation of an advertisement to share with the class

ACTIVITY FIVE:

Advertisng Appeals

Objectives: to identify examples of a variety of advertising appeals in television, radio, or printed ads, and to rewrite an advertisement by replacing advertising appeals with more factual information

Materials: student-provided example of one or more advertisements, or printed ads from magazines and newspapers

paper and pencils

Procedure: When goods and services are advertised, certain appeals are made to the consumer. Challenge your students to:

1. find an example of television, radio, magazine, newspaper, or billboard ads that use the following appeals.

2. rewrite an advertisement using more factual information than appears in a given ad.

Advertising Appeals

1. *Brand loyalty:* The advertiser wants you to continue buying the established brands, especially those from older, well-established businesses.

2. *Conformity:* The bandwagon approach. "Everybody" is buying this particular brand or item so you should too.

3. *Hero worship:* Endorsement of a product by a big name in entertainment or sports.

4. *Status:* An appeal to the buyer's class-consciousness.

5. *Humor:* Entertaining, but deceptive; says little about the product.

6. *Feminine attractiveness:* A wishful-thinking ad, appealing to girls or women who wish to be more beautiful, sexy, and alluring.

7. *Masculine attractiveness:* Same kind of appeal as number 6; an appeal to the he-man image.

8. *Style changes:* The buyer is asked to keep up with the times. This may include fad items.

9. *Vanity:* This kind of ad appeals to the buyer's self-image or ego gratification. The buyer's happiness is placed first in importance.

10. *Economy:* Everyone likes to think he or she can economize while spending.

11. *Luxury:* Symbols of wealth and excess.

12. *Convenience:* Work-saver and time-saver devices.

13. *Creativity:* Buyer can add a personal touch to the product's use.

14. *Security:* This covers many kinds of security—emotional, social, and financial.

15. *Sex:* The ad appeals to the lure of sex. It is very similar to the appeals of numbers 6 and 7.

There are also combinations of appeals, and more than one appeal may appear in an ad.

Analysis of Advertising

1. How does the ad explain the real features or advantages of the product?

2. Does the ad compare with that of a competitive item?

3. Are there any meaningless or "puff" words added?

4. What specific appeals to the buyer does the ad make?

Evaluation: correct identification of a variety of advertising appeals from verbally or visually presented ads, completion of rewritten advertisement, correct answers to Analysis of Advertising questions

UNIT EVALUATION: POSTERS

Have students work in pairs to make posters about being wise consumers. Posters each should include at least one slogan, two facts, one opinion, and three visuals, or other criteria appropriate for your class. Finished products should look something like the figure on page 80 and be displayed throughout the classroom or school. This project can be used with any unit.

ADDITIONAL ACTIVITIES

Extension and Evaluation

1. Replicate Activities Three through Five using other nonconsumable products or consumable products such as peanut butter, chocolate-chip cookies, or popcorn.

2. Have students do some comparison shopping. Collect copies of newspapers from the day your area grocery stores run their large ads. Instruct each student to choose a single food item and find the best buy and where it can be found. Be sure students consider the unit price rather than just the list price of the item.

3. Since a large part of being a consumer involves spending money, it might be appropriate to include activities involving the identification of coins, making change, and writing checks during this unit. Skills with decimal computation could also be taught or reviewed.

4. Build reading skills in skimming and finding details through the use of classified ads. Assign specific or general features to be identified, and instruct students to find these by skimming through the ads. You might then encourage them to write their own ads including these details or features.

5. Use a book such as *Advertising* (Greenhaven Press, 1991) to further examine the topic of advertising.

6. Have students investigate whether the Internet uses advertising and to explain their findings. If yes, how is it used? If no, how could it be used?

Teacher Resources

See Appendix B for resources and addresses.

TIME

What Time Is It? The concept of time is presented in a broader context than is usually found in school curricula. Earth's rotation, pendula, sundials, and clocks are all used to measure the passage of time.

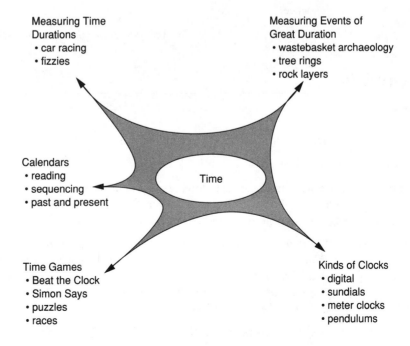

Measuring Time
Durations
• car racing
• fizzies

Measuring Events of
Great Duration
• wastebasket archaeology
• tree rings
• rock layers

Calendars
• reading
• sequencing
• past and present

Time

Time Games
• Beat the Clock
• Simon Says
• puzzles
• races

Kinds of Clocks
• digital
• sundials
• meter clocks
• pendulums

INTRODUCTION

Time has been described as a flowing river, and as a fixed set of points through which we pass. Whatever it is, it plays an important part in everyone's life. This thematic unit centers around time, its measurement, and its application to simple situations that are familiar to children.

Following a pretest and the presentation of some introductory information are seven activities, which are presented in a logical sequence. You may wish to combine two activities together or extend one over several days. As children evidence interest, you will want to direct them to some of the independent investigations.

Unit Objectives. Students will:

1. demonstrate an understanding of sun time.

2. demonstrate an understanding of how early clocks were synchronized with the sun.

3. become familiar with other time-measuring devices (e.g., candles, water clocks, and pendulums).

4. correctly calculate lapsed time.

5. correctly order events according to time sequence.

6. demonstrate a preliminary feel for very short and very great time durations.

Appropriate Grade Levels. Elementary and Middle School

Vocabulary.

revolution	rotation
synchronize	sundial
lapse	quartz
sequence	axis

Note: See Appendix A for planning sheets.

ACTIVITY ONE:

Survey

Objective: to measure time concepts before unit implementation

Materials: paper and pencils

Procedure: Have your class read the following story, or read it to them, and have them answer the questions that follow it. This will serve as a standard by which you can later measure the learning that has occurred through completion of the unit.

> *The station wagon stopped at the fishing pier. Nancy, Bill, and their dad got out. The children took their fishing poles and ran on the noisy boards to the end of the pier. Dad brought the bucket of worms with him. As he set it down he said, "I will be back to get you at 3 o'clock this afternoon." "What time is it now?" asked Nancy. "It's 10 o'clock in the morning," he said.*

1. For how many hours can Nancy and Bill fish?

2. Will it be dark when their dad picks them up?

3. They don't have a watch. How could they tell when it is about 3 o'clock?

4. Their fishing box contains hooks, sinkers, lines, shiny little spoons, and artificial worms. Which of these could be used to make a time-measuring device? Draw a picture showing how you would make it.

Evaluation: correct answers given to the four questions

ACTIVITY TWO:

Introduction

Objective: to present preliminary information concerning time and time measurement

Materials: none required, although examples of a variety of time measurement devices may be useful

Procedure: In a discussion, or by the use of a film, present some of the ideas that follow. Eliciting as many as possible from students' acquired knowledge will generally be preferable to lecturing to them. It is important that students are exposed to this information during the course of the introductory discussion.

Time Information

People began developing time units and measuring durations by making comparisons with the positions and (apparent) movement of the sun across the sky. When the sun was visible, it was daytime; after the sun set it became night. Later, people watched shadows move, constructed sundials, and noted that the shadows were shortest when the sun was overhead. They also noticed that at noon, winter shadows were much longer than at noon during the summer. Morning, noon, end-of-day, and seasons were "invented." Sundials were refined with markings so that the passage of an hour could be measured. Later, mechanical devices (candles, water clocks, and mechanical clocks) were invented. They "ran" at the same speed as the sundial, and had the added advantage of telling time on cloudy days and at night. History records the development of astronomical instruments, refined clocks, and watches, the discovery of the pendulum, and an increasing ability to measure the duration of events with precision.

Over the years, sundials and water clocks were replaced by clocks with escapements (ticking devices) and pendulums. These are being replaced today with electronic devices containing a tiny crystal of vibrating quartz, printed circuits, and light-emitting numerical readouts.

We can relate to events that have durations of seconds, minutes, hours, days, months, and quite a few years. It is easier to relate to shorter events measured in seconds, minutes, and sometimes hours. The ability to conceive of duration decreases as we deal with events of great duration such as geological eras, which may extend over millions of years, and events of very short duration, such as the single vibration of the quartz crystal, or the duration of a single computer calculation measured in nanoseconds (millionths of a second).

Time-measuring devices provide two distinct kinds of information. First, these devices show what time it is at that moment. Second, they can tell us the length of duration of an event. To measure such a duration, one records the time at the beginning and at the end of an event and then subtracts. If, for example, Jim started to mow the lawn at 2:00 P.M. and finished at 3:30 P.M., the duration would be: $3:30 - 2:00 = 1:30$. One could, instead, count up from the first event and end at the second event: 2:00 to 3:00 (1 hr.) to 3:30 (½ hr.)= 1½ hours. To avoid the subtraction or addition steps, we could wait until the hands are at zero (12 o'clock) and then start the event. Stop watches work this way: When you press the button, the hands instantly move to zero.

Note: You may wish to check and see that all children understand how to read clock faces. If children have problems, use a take-apart clock face and begin with the hour hand, then the minute hand, and then a combination.

Evaluation: none needed directly, except perhaps relative to the final note concerning clock-reading skills

ACTIVITY THREE:

"Built-In" Clocks

Objective: to present the concept of "built-in" time, and to provide opportunities to measure individual accuracy of it

Materials: a watch or small clock

slips of paper and pencils

Procedure: Begin by covering the face of a clock. Select one child to be the clock watcher. Set the clock at zero (12:00) and begin reading a short story. The clock watcher should have small slips of paper and a pencil. Tell the children to listen to the story and not look at the clock. When they think 5 minutes have elapsed, they should raise a hand. Have the clock watcher give a card to each child as hands go up. On the card the clock watcher writes the elapsed time in minutes (2, 3, 4, etc.). When all children have a card, have all the children with the lowest number form a line. Do the same in succession for the other numbers. With the children in lines, explain how they form a graph. Then draw a grid like the one shown in Figure 3.6 on the chalkboard. Enter the number of children guessing 2, 3, and so on. Call the children's attention to the most guessed time, shortest guessed time, number of people guessing 5 minutes, etc.

Help children read the graph by asking questions such as the following:

1. How many guessed 2 minutes? How many minutes off were they?

2. How many minutes was the longest time-duration guess?

3. Did anyone guess (pick one that no one guessed) 12 minutes?

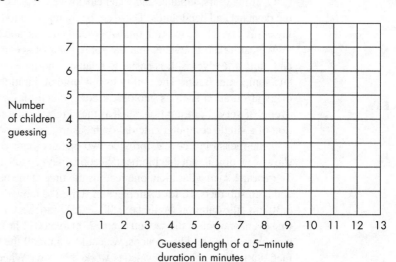

FIGURE 3.6
Built-in time measurement graph

4. If we used Mary for our clock (Mary guessed 3 minutes), would we go to lunch early or late?

5. If we used John (suppose John raised his hand at 7 minutes) as our clock and we agreed that he told the right time, would the real clock be said to run fast or slow?

Encourage children to work in pairs. Have them practice guessing 1-, 2-, and even 3-minute intervals. Have them do this by having one child guess with eyes closed while the other watches the clock. If time allows, bring children together and repeat the first activity. Compare the two graphs. Have children discuss whether or not the practice of guessing elapsed time improves the accuracy of the guess.

Evaluation: completion of graphs, active participation in guessing activities

ACTIVITY FOUR:

Making and Using Clocks

Objective: to identify daily events according to time of occurrence

Materials: paper plates and brads, or prepared plate clocks (one per child)

Procedure: Children rarely know when events in their lives occur. Poll the class to find out when they think they do the following:

get up in the morning

leave home for school (or to catch the school bus)

start the school day (first bell rings)

go to lunch

leave school in the afternoon

have the evening meal

go to bed on school nights

For each question, have children set clocks. Have them do so by using paper plate clocks they have made themselves or that have been prepared for them. You may wish to have one row of children per question line up from earliest to latest time for each of the events.

Note: At this point, you may wish to use the clocks for some skills practice in translating spoken time to a clock face configuration and vice versa. This will give you an opportunity to do some diagnostic work and assign additional practice as needed by individual students.

Evaluation: ability to identify accurate or near-accurate times for daily events, completion of take-home activity and class time-telling activities, correct completion of paper-plate clock if assigned

ACTIVITY FIVE:

Day and Night

Objective: to understand how day and night are caused by the rotation of Earth

Materials: globe and/or white ball   small stick

clay   direct light source (e.g., flashlight or lamp)

Procedure: If children have not done globe and map work, begin by holding up a globe and explaining how, each day, Earth makes one full turn or rotation on its axis. Turn off all but one light or close all but one shade. Slowly rotate the globe. Ask the children where it is day and where it is night. Locate your city (or state) on the globe. Identify it with a lump of clay. Turn the globe so that the "sun" is directly over the clay. Rotate the globe so the sun appears to set in the west. Continue rotating the globe until the sun appears to rise in the east. Have children guess what time it is when the sun is in various positions in relationship to the lump of clay.

A second and similar activity works best if you have a white ball. Again, fasten a lump of clay to the ball or globe and repeat the rotation. Then fasten a vertical stick about 5 cm long into the clay. Have children watch the shadow of the stick as the globe or ball is turned. Through questions, relate the position of the shadow to the time of day. Then relate the globe or ball to Earth and the clay to the region where the school and the playground are located. Ask, "What would happen if, instead of erecting the stick on the globe, we erected a pole on the playground?" Finish by explaining to the class that their next-day's activity will be to find out the answer to this question.

Evaluation: ability to correctly answer questions, either verbally or in writing, concerning the causes of day and night and how shadows are changed or affected by Earth's rotation

ACTIVITY SIX:

Shadow Movement

Objective: to watch and record the movement of shadows

Materials: stick or pole, about 1 meter long

10 rocks

marker

Procedure: Start this activity first thing in the morning. After briefly reviewing the findings and explorations of Activity Five, have children erect a pole about 1 meter high on a sunny spot on the playground. At exactly 9:00 A.M. place a rock at the tip of the shadow of the pole. Have a student write the number 9 on the rock. Plan your schedule so that each hour children can go to the playground to place and label a new stone. Shortly before dismissal time, make a final visit to their sundial, noting the positions of the rocks. Discuss the experience.

Evaluation: completion of group activity, ability to verbally relate findings to the passage and measurement of time

ACTIVITY SEVEN:

Recording Clock Times

Objective: to teach skills relative to the recording of clock time and time durations

Materials: paper-plate clocks

worksheets or paper for recording times

Procedure: This activity is designed to introduce clock recording skills and duration measurement skills. Children will need previously made paper-plate clock faces and worksheets for recording.

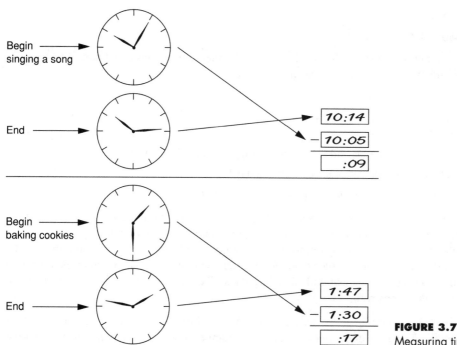

FIGURE 3.7
Measuring time durations

Begin with a clock face with an hour hand only. Have children record various face configurations on the worksheet. Remove the hour hand and put on a minute hand. Have children again record various configurations. Some time must be spent explaining the two number lines on the clock's face. Then combine the two hands and show children that recording time is a matter of reading the two hand positions separately. Point out that when the hour hand is between two numbers, the smaller number is recorded. Ask whether there is an exception to this rule. If no answer is given by a student, point out that when the hand is between 12 and 1, the 12 is recorded.

This is a good time to compare clock faces with digital clocks. Children will recognize that a digital readout eliminates the conversion from hand configuration to number.

When measuring time durations, children record the time on the worksheet at the beginning and at the end of the event. To simplify the substraction process, the ending time is recorded in the top box and the beginning time is recorded under it, as shown in Figure 3.7. Another method is to count ahead from the time the activity begins until the time it is finished. For example, if the activity begins at 10:05, children may count the nine minutes until 10:14 (10:06, 10:07, 10:08, etc.).

Evaluation: correct identification and recording of clock times and correct calculation of elapsed times

ACTIVITY EIGHT:

Calendar Time

Objective: to relate clock time to calendar time, and to build skills and awareness of the concepts and identification of *week* and *month*

Materials: large calendars

7-day strips

Procedure: Bring several large calendars to class. Begin by asking questions about days. For example, you might ask the following questions:

1. How long is a day?
2. When does a day start? End?
3. Why are days given seven different names? (You may wish to point out the 7-day sequence of names, and the religious origins of this 7-day unit.)
4. What part of the calendar represents a day?
5. How can we tell the name of any particular day?

Make up a number of 7-day strips. Explain how each strip represents a week: It begins with Sunday and ends with Saturday. Perhaps some children would like to find out about the origins of the names given to days. Assemble the 7-day strips to form a month of 4 weeks. Ask children to name some months. Ask them to name the month of their birthday and lay out a large calendar with class birthdays. You may choose to relate various holidays to the calendar as well.

Evaluation: active participation in group activity, subsequent ability to identify, verbally or in writing, days of the week, number of days in a week, number of weeks in a month, names of some months of the year and month of his or her birthday

UNIT EVALUATION: ACCORDIAN BOOK

Have students make individual accordian books to explain what they have learned about time. Give each student a yard of adding machine paper to divide into 12 sections, as shown in Figure 3.8. Section 1 is the cover. One key fact about time should be written in each section from 2 through 11. Illustration can be included. Section 12 should be used for the student to identify the three best things about the unit. An accordian book can be used for any unit evaluation.

ADDITIONAL ACTIVITIES:

Extension and Evaluation

1. *Battery, spring, or fly-wheel driven cars* can be raced along a marked track. Floor tiles provide convenient distance marks. Encourage children to run one car at a time over a uniform distance. The lapsed time, which can be measured with a 1-second pendulum, allows children to report their car's speed. Children can redesign cars for increased speed or distance.

2. *Fizzies or Alka Seltzer* tablets, when dropped in water, release bubbles of carbon dioxide. The tablets contain a dry mixture of sodium bicarbonate and citric acid plus other ingredients for flavor and digestive aid. The rate at which they react is related to the temperature of the water. Children can measure the fizz time in water of various temperatures.

3. *Beat the Clock* was a popular television game in which contestants were challenged to perform certain tasks in a given time. Points were gained for early completion

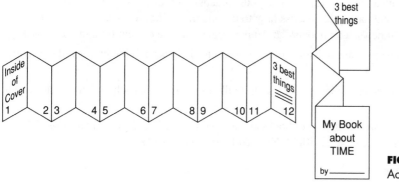

FIGURE 3.8
Accordian book

and lost if contestants were unable to beat the clock. Children can come up with a variety of Beat the Clock contests. For example, you might try nail driving, card sorting, transferring liquid from one jar to another with a spoon, blowing up balloons, threading several needles or beads, or stacking dominos, blocks, or Tinkertoy connecters.

4. *Early time-keeping devices* can be researched by children. Humans have developed many ingenious devices to determine time of day, day of the month, and month of the year. The following words can be used as keys for dictionary, encyclopedia, and reference book research:

sundial	escapement	zodiacal constellations
water clock	sidereal time	pole star
pendulum	horology	Big Dipper
	observatory	

5. *Wastebasket archeology* simulates the procedures used by archeologists in excavating digs. The concept of sequential deposition applies to trash thrown in a wastebasket, to artifacts thrown onto garbage dumps, and to stratas of sediment deposited by water that has eroded and transported rocks, sand, and soil. Wastebaskets can be secured from several places such as other classrooms, secretaries' offices, stores, and professional offices. Encourage children to lay out a table top into four areas and remove about one quarter of the contents of a basket at a time. The first pile is labeled "late afternoon," the next "early afternoon," then "late morning," and finally "early morning." Rummaging for interesting items and clues will not interfere too seriously with the development of a chart representing items and order of deposition. Have the children reconstruct a scenario describing the source of the basket, the habits of the people using it, and a chronology of their activities during the day.

    Other systems made up of layers deposited over time include tree rings, rock layers, rust and corrosion on metals, barnacles encrusted on sunken ships, and snow and dirt layers that can be detected by cutting through banks or drifts of snow with a shovel. These can also be examined and used to develop concepts of time passage.

6. Construct a pendulum. Have students explore the operations of the pendulum and relate these to time.

7. Investigate a Time Zone map with your students. Introduce the prime meridian and the international date line. Discuss how to use the map. Choose world news articles from your local newspaper and ask students to figure out the current time in each place.

8. Have students make a display of various kinds of clocks or a bulletin board of pictures of clocks.

9. Invite a jeweler to visit your class and talk about his or her job and about clocks and watches.

10. Make a classroom display of books about time, such as *The Super Science Book of Time* by K. Davies and W. Oldfield, New York: Thomson, 1993.

Teacher Resources

See Appendix B for resources and addresses.

CHANGE: Growing and Using Plants

Growing and Using Plants: Weight, volume, length, temperature, and area are all incorporated in applied settings in this measurement-oriented theme. This unit will be of special interest to the amateur gardener and to students who have a green thumb.

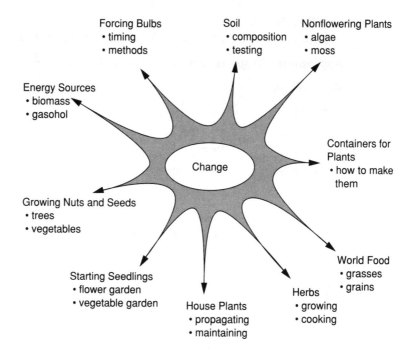

Forcing Bulbs
• timing
• methods

Soil
• composition
• testing

Nonflowering Plants
• algae
• moss

Energy Sources
• biomass
• gasohol

Containers for Plants
• how to make them

Growing Nuts and Seeds
• trees
• vegetables

Change

World Food
• grasses
• grains

Starting Seedlings
• flower garden
• vegetable garden

House Plants
• propagating
• maintaining

Herbs
• growing
• cooking

INTRODUCTION

This theme is planned to give children who have some knowledge of seed germination an opportunity to explore many ways that plants are propagated and used. The theme incorporates plant growth studies, record keeping, cooking activities, simple pottery making, container art, sugar fermentation studies, distillation procedures, and a variety of plant growth and propagation activities.

Plants and animals form a mutual support system, although most plants will grow in the absence of animals. The selection, hybridization, development, and cultivation of plants for man's use is the single-most important resource-producing industry in the world. Agriculture makes us think of fields of wheat, corn, or alfalfa, but the process of cultivation applies to the growth of a wide variety of plants for shade and beauty as well as for forest and agriculture products.

This theme deals with a few of the many ways in which people can use plants. It can be easily expanded to include children developing a corner of the school grounds into an environmental center, setting up a small yard and garden sales center, constructing a window greenhouse in the classroom, or starting a houseplant boutique.

As the world's population increases, production of food must keep pace. Food plays a major role in the trade of products among nations. Whether children become commodity traders, grow food commercially, or just use their knowledge as a way of raising a backyard garden or beautifying their home, the theme is of immediate concern to them.

Unit Objectives. Students will:

1. become aware of the many ways in which people use plants and plant products.

2. grow a variety of plants from seeds and cuttings.

3. be able to name some of the components of soil.

4. make pots and containers in which to grow plants.

5. learn about and grow both flowering and nonflowering plants.

Appropriate Grade Levels. Elementary and Middle School

Vocabulary.

biomass	cutting
gasohol	sterilize
organism	flats
propagate	vermiculite
moss	seedling
algae	

Note: See Appendix A for planning sheets.

ACTIVITY ONE:

Introducing the Theme

Objective: to introduce students to the theme of the unit

Materials: filmstrip, videotape, or book of your choice

Procedure: Choose a filmstrip, videotape, or book dealing with the production and use of plant products. Any one you choose can be used to initiate a class discussion because most children have planted seeds, know about plant growth, and have some background information and interest. Ask children to brainstorm about the many kinds and uses of plants. Have them think of a normal day in their lives and what part plants and plant products play in it.

   The webbing diagram at the beginning of the unit is for your use, although it is likely that you will want to use it directly with your class as well. The activities presented in this unit are intended to provide suggestions, ideas, and guidance. As with other themes, encourage your children to identify and explore topics of high interest to them. Group sharing by means of reports, posters, and minibooks should be encouraged.

Evaluation: attention to, and participation in discussion

ACTIVITY TWO:

Testing Soil for Organisms

Objective: to test garden soil for the presence of organisms

Materials: funnel

   light bulb

   jar

   garden soil

   instant baby cereal

   small plastic container

   toothpicks

Procedure: Explain to your class that it is unwise to use soil directly from the garden because it may contain organisms that will eat or otherwise harm plants. Therefore, soil should be sterilized. Suggest to students that it might be interesting to test the soil for the presence of organisms before sterilizing it. This is done using a funnel, a light bulb, and a jar.

   Help your students follow these steps:

1. Place the garden soil in the funnel, then set the funnel in the jar with a bit of water in the bottom.

2. Hang a light bulb over the funnel as close to the soil as possible. Heat from the bulb will force the larger organisms out of the funnel and into the water, where they can be observed.

3. Tiny soil organisms called nematodes can be cultured from a soil sample using instant baby cereal. Mix an individual serving-size package of cereal and add a teaspoon of soil to it. Place the mixture in a small plastic container with a cover. A shallow plastic box works very well.

4. In a day or two, condensation will form on the underside of the lid. Remove a drop of the liquid with a toothpick and examine it with a microscope. Nematodes are tiny, often nearly transparent worms that inhabit soil, water, and many other organisms.

Evaluation: successful completion of the tests described, with active participation observed

ACTIVITY THREE:

Preparing the Soil

Objective: to sterilize and otherwise prepare garden soil for indoor planting

Materials: garden soil

cake pans

sand, humus, or vermiculite

Procedure: An easy way to sterilize soil is to place it in a cake pan and bake it in an oven. Set the oven controls at 250°F and bake the soil for several hours or overnight. If an oven is available, you may choose to do this at school. Otherwise, you should bake the soil at home the evening before.

For successful planting, the soil should be soft and friable. Have your students test for proper consistency by taking handfuls of moist soil and squeezing them into balls. If, as they open their hands, the soil breaks apart, it is satisfactory. If it sticks together and packs, it can be loosened by adding sand, humus, or one of several soil conditioners such as vermiculite to it. You also can use vermiculite (an insulation material made from mica) by itself for most planting needs if obtaining or sterilizing soil is not possible. Vermiculite is available in sacks at building material stores, as well as at garden stores. If you use vermiculite alone, you should add a bit of fertilizer (liquid or solid) occasionally.

Evaluation: completion of suitable planting soil mixture

ACTIVITY FOUR:

Planting Flats

Objective: to make planting flats

Materials: small cardboard boxes

plastic, preferably clear

vermiculite or sand

Procedure: Planting flats can be made from small cardboard boxes that have been cut down to about a 3-inch depth and lined with clear plastic. Flats are handy for starting seedlings and conducting investigations. Since the purpose of the plastic is to keep the cardboard dry, drainage can be a problem. If you put an inch of vermiculite, or sand, in the bottom of the flat before adding soil, and if you water only when the surface of the soil begins to dry out, the problem can be overcome.

Help your students prepare their flats. It is always wise to have more materials than will be needed for the finished products to allow room for errors. While any size and shape of box can be used, you may wish to have students save their empty milk cartons from lunch.

Evaluation: successful completion of planting flats

ACTIVITY FIVE:

Pots and Containers

Objective: to make one or more pots or containers for planting

Materials: dependent upon type(s) of pots to be made (see individual sections of the activity for specifics)

Procedure: Clay pots and plants go hand-in-hand. A 10-pound bag of clay from the local pottery supplier and many hands to pinch pots will produce an assortment of 20 to 50 containers, depending on size and wall thickness. If your school has a kiln, you are in business. If not, discuss the problem with the pottery supply person. Ask about clays that can be baked at low temperatures. In some cases, bisque, or low-temperature firing, can be done in an ordinary oven.

Directions follow for making a variety of pots. You and your students can make as few or as many of these as you desire. If you make more than one kind, several days will be needed to complete the activity.

Pinch Pots

Pinch pots are simple pots made without the use of a wheel or mold. Have students begin with a ball of clay about 2 inches in diameter. Students should slowly fashion the clay into a pot shape. Tell them that pots that taper from the bottom to the top are easy to work with and fine for plants. Encourage the children to keep pot walls uniform in thickness as much as possible. Note: Clay should never be rinsed down a sink drain. Students should wipe off excess clay from their fingers before washing up.

Coil Pots

Long, snakelike pieces of clay are used to fashion coil pots. Students should start with a 1-inch ball of clay, rolling the clay carefully into a uniform snake about 12 inches long. They should then wind and coil the snake, forming the bottom and then the sides of the pot. Once it is formed, they should carefully press the bottom and then the sides of the pot together using fingers and thumb. A lightly moistened sponge can be used to smooth and even the pot.

Charming pots can also be made from several separate coils of clay. Your students should start by making six coils, each about 2 inches in diameter. Placing the first coil on a flat surface, they should then arrange the other coils to form the side walls. Tell them not to worry if a few small gaps remain between the coils. A long snake can be added to form the top of the pot. A bit of careful pinching and a light wipe with a moist sponge will ready the pot for drying.

Containers from Sheets of Clay

Planting containers can also be made by using a rolling pin to form a sheet of clay. If the clay sticks to the pin, have students roll it out between two sheets of foil or plastic wrap. When they have an 8-inch disc of clay, the edges can be slanted upward, forming a saucer or pan. A 10-by-10-inch rectangle can be formed into a tray by the same process.

Papier-mâché Pots

To begin making papier-mâché pots, have students mix torn newsprint and water in a bucket. They should then let the mixture soak for several days until the paper comes apart. At this point, they should be instructed to vigorously stir the mixture or work it with their hands. When the paper is almost all in fine shreds, help your students drain off some of the water and add a tablespoon of powdered wallpaper paste. Have each student select a glass jar that is a bit wider at the top than the bottom. They should take some of the papier-mâché and form it over the jar, squeezing out the water as they work. Once the papier-mâché pot is formed, have students set their pots aside for several hours, but not long enough for them to dry completely. Then help them very carefully slide the pot off the glass form. Later, additional papier-mâché can be added once the pot has dried. A lip or raised designs can be added. Paint and varnish can be used to give the paper pot a moderate degree of water resistance. If desired, the inside of the pot can be coated with hot paraffin.

Small pots for transplanting can be made from a papier-mâché base. In this case, try soft toweling or bathroom tissue. Have students completely shred the paper in the water, adding enough paper so the mixture is about the consistency of thin batter (slurry). Each student then should cut a piece of screen wire and form a small pot shape, then pour the paper slurry through the screen pot form until the inside of the form is thinly coated with paper. When this is done, students should gently squeeze the moisture from the paper and allow it to dry. Once dry, a slight spreading of the screen will make it possible to remove the light paper pot. Students should then trim the top and set the little pots aside to dry. Plants started in these containers can be planted directly in the garden, container and all.

Other Containers

Children can make many other containers. Baby food jars can be painted or trimmed with paper. Cans can be cut with tin snips to form handles and curled edges. Containers can be flocked by painting them with glue, varnish, or shellac and then rolling them in sand, vermiculite, or sawdust. Encourage creative and artistic expressions by children. Some may wish to make hanging pots, some animal-shaped pots, and some animal heads with deep furrows in which rye grass can be planted.

Evaluation: successful completion of one or more pots

ACTIVITY SIX:

Growing Grasses and Grains

Objective: to plant and grow grass or seed grains

Materials: variety of grass and grain seeds

flats or pots filled with soil

opaque plastic

stick frame for plastic

Procedure: Arrange for your class to visit a farm or seed store where bulk seed is sold. Bring along a dozen little plastic bags with labels and purchase a tablespoon of each of a variety of seeds. Rye grass, oats, corn, millet, and alfalfa all grow vigorously and germinate quickly. Encourage children to try many kinds of seeds.

The seeds can be planted in flats or pots. Give your students this general seed depth planting rule: Soil should cover the seed by no more than four times the seed's longest dimension. Tell them that very tiny seeds can be mixed with soil, and this mixture then sprinkled evenly over the soil in the flat and patted down. Tell the class that flats should never dry out during germination, but neither should they be overly moist. One of the better ways of keeping the soil surface moist is to cover the flat with thin opaque plastic until the seeds show signs of germination. Then build a frame over the flat with sticks or Tinkertoys and hang a clear plastic cover over the flat.

After germination has been checked, seeds can be planted in rows in the flats. Have students label each row carefully so that they can remember what was planted. It would be useful to make a class growth-rate chart for each variety.

Evaluation: successful growing of planted seeds, and completion of a growth chart marking their progress

ACTIVITY SEVEN:

Growing and Cooking with Herbs

Objective: to grow a variety of herbs and use them in cooking

Materials: variety of herb seeds

flats or containers filled with soil

cooking equipment and ingredients as desired

plastic cups

gauze

aluminum foil

Procedure: Most hardware and seed stores carry collections of herb seeds. Included in the collection are packages such as rosemary, mint, chives, basil, thyme, and parsley. Have the children follow planting instructions on the packages. All will grow well in flats. Warn the children that many herbs are slow to germinate, with some seeds taking as much as two weeks to sprout.

Collecting recipes using herbs can be an interesting library or resource activity to pursue while the class is waiting for the seeds to grow. Parents, grandparents, and neighbors can be consulted as well. Encourage your children to make a collection of herbs and spices and to find out about them: on what part of the plant they grow and which parts of the plant are edible. Have children make fragrance boxes, which can be used to teach them to recognize many herbs and spices by their aroma. Such a box can be made from a small plastic cup, a bit of moist gauze, and a foil cover.

Evaluation: growth of herb seeds planted, cooking or collecting recipes for herbs, and correct identification of several herbs in fragrance boxes

ACTIVITY EIGHT:

Propagating House Plants by Cuttings

Objective: to grow plants from houseplant cuttings

Materials: cuttings of common houseplants

containers filled with sand or vermiculite

pots filled with soil

Procedure: Most varieties of green, vinelike houseplants can be snipped and rooted with comparative ease. Philodendrons, pothos, ivy, and fleshy-leaved plants such as Swedish ivy all root well. The trick is to root fairly short end cuttings. A good rule is to count leaves from the tip of the shoot and snip between the third and fifth leaf. We suggest that you make the cuttings at home and bring them to class. Cuttings can be put by students in well-drained pots with washed sand or can be rooted in vermiculite in paper or plastic cups with a hole in the bottom for drainage.

Several plants, including spider plants, air plants, begonia, and African violets, can be propagated from leaf cuttings. Have students start with a flat filled with clean sand or vermiculite. Have them place the leaf rib-side down slightly into the sand (some gardeners snip the middle rib in one or two places). Make sure students keep their flats moist and covered with plastic so the sand or vermiculite is always slightly moist. Tiny new plants will soon appear at the leaf margins. They can be removed by students and planted in pots when they have four leaves.

Evaluation: plant grown from rooted cutting

ACTIVITY NINE:

Starting Seedlings

Objective: to successfully start seedlings from seeds

Materials: variety of flower or vegetable seeds   flats filled with soil

Procedure: The success of the amateur gardener depends on his or her ability to start plants from seed early in the spring. Only through experience do children learn which plants can be started indoors, which ones to transplant to pots, and how to harden them before planting them in the garden. Seed packages provide general planting and growing information. Some packages suggest that seeds be sown indoors to start and others recommend that seeds be planted directly in the garden. Many seed companies will send seed catalogs free or for postage and handling costs.

Children can start single rows of various vegetables and flowers in flats. When plants have sprouted and four to six tiny leaves appear, they can be carefully transplanted into other flats or little pots. One of the common mistakes of the beginner is letting plants in flats grow too close together. If you don't want to transplant rows that are too thick, have students pull out plants (this is called thinning) so there is an inch between each plant left in the flat. Although plants vary from region to region, here are a few that guarantee success and that children may wish to try.

Vegetables	*Flowers*
tomatoes, cabbage, broccoli,	petunias, portulaca, alyssum,
eggplant, hybrid bush melons,	verbena, calendula, snapdragons,
green peppers, cauliflower	marigolds

Large vegetables, root vegetables, most vines, corn, sunflowers, zinnias, sweet peas, and morning glories can be started indoors in pots. Encourage children to try any plant they wish since that is how one learns the skills of the amateur gardener.

Evaluation: successful growth of one or more plants started from seeds

ACTIVITY TEN:

Starting Plants from Nuts and Fruit Seeds

Objective: to start plants from fruit seeds or nuts, and to learn that processed seeds will not grow

Materials: variety of fruit seeds or nuts

variety of seed-containing processed foods

containers filled with soil

Procedure: Many interesting house plants and trees can be started from nuts or seeds taken from fruit. You may ask students to bring in seeds or you might bring them to school yourself. In the case of fruit, the seeds should be removed and washed carefully. They should be allowed to dry for a few days. Such fresh fruit as apricots, peaches, pears, apples, oranges, tangerines, lemons, limes, grapefruits, avocadoes, and grapes can be tried.

Nuts, too, will germinate but may pose some difficulties. Some must be frozen for a few weeks to induce germination, while others may require several months to germinate. Raw peanuts can be purchased from a health food store. Seeds from roasted peanuts, like those of cooked fruit, will not germinate.

You may also want to have children plant seeds found in cans of fruits or vegetables. Let them try these seeds and discover that the preserving process and the associated heat kills seeds.

Well-drained, sandy soil seems to be the best choice for fruit seed germination. Once the little plants have sprouted, they can be potted to make attractive houseplants. All of these plants need abundant sunlight. Be aware that the germination time for citrus seeds, avocados, and nuts may be as much as six weeks. For this reason, this activity might well be selected by a group that has another activity underway.

Evaluation: successful growing of plants from the seeds or nuts provided, knowledge gained of some conditions necessary for seed growth

ACTIVITY ELEVEN:

Biomass and Gasohol

Objective: to learn about plant-produced energy sources, and to complete one or more activities producing gasohol

Materials: seeds, as appropriate (see Procedure)   5-gallon bucket and cloth for cover

large pan   yeast

algae   pressure cooker and hot plate

fertilizer   pan

instruments to measure weight   rubber or plastic tubing

syrup or molasses

Procedure: As we approach the 21st century, we face a time when world petroleum resources will be far below those of today and prices will be much higher. Many people have begun to search for alternative energy sources for home heating, vehicle propulsion, and the powering of some industries. Two interesting plant possibilities are biomass and gasohol.

Provide your class with the following background information. All parts of plants, roots, stems, and leaves are made up of a high percentage of cellulose. Cellulose is a chemical in the same group with sugar and starch and will burn. Plants produce sugars, starches, and cellulose using sunlight as the powering source, and water from the soil and carbon dioxide from the air as basic raw materials. The process from plant to plant varies in efficiency.

Many studies are underway to measure the amount of burnable material produced by plants per unit of growing area.

Children can conduct similar studies by marking off areas and planting such high biomass producers as corn and sunflowers. Another simple plant to study, which under some conditions is an efficient biomass producer, is algae. To grow algae, fill a large pan with water, add a small amount of fertilizer, and set it in a sunny spot. A small amount of shredded algae should be added. In a week or 10 days the algae should be strained from the water, dried, and weighed. From their data, children can now make estimates of what weight of biomass could be produced in a large pond or lake.

Gasohol is made by adding about 10% alcohol to 90% gasoline. Though this does not seem like much of a gasoline saving, children can calculate how much gasoline could be saved in a year by their family, their community, and their state if gasohol were used in place of gasoline. Gasoline consumption figures are readily available from state transportation and energy departments.

The alcohol that is added to gasoline is usually made from grain that has a high sugar content. Sugar cane, sugar beets, and corn can be used. Children can explore the fermentation process by using molasses or dark syrup. Help them mix about 1 cup of syrup or molasses with 2 quarts of water and put the mixture in a 5-gallon bucket. Then add a package of yeast. Explain to your students that yeast is a plant that has no chlorophyll and cannot manufacture its food by photosynthesis. Yeast uses sugar for its growth energy and in the process gives off carbon dioxide, water, and alcohol (known as ethanol or grain alcohol). Make sure that they keep the bucket at room temperature and keep a damp cloth over the top of the bucket. In a short time, the children will see a froth of carbon dioxide bubbles forming over the liquid. Allow the yeast mixture to ferment for several days. Explain that the odor is not carbon dioxide but is other gases and wastes produced by the yeast.

If you wish to have your class distill some alcohol from the mixture, an easy way is to use a small pressure cooker. Students should pour 2 inches of the liquid into the pressure cooker, which should then be covered and placed in a pan of water on an electric hot plate. Do not put the pressure gauge on, but instead attach a long rubber hose or plastic tube to the pipe on the top of the cooker. Use a candy thermometer and heat the water in the pan to about 160° to 180°F. Do not let the water in the pan boil. As soon as the liquid in the pressure cooker gets hot (about 20 to 30 minutes) alcohol will evaporate from the liquid, travel into the tubing, and condense. The drops coming from the tubing will contain a fairly high percent of alcohol.

For this last procedure, be sure that you carefully follow these safety precautions:

1. Use an electric hot plate on low heat. Do not use an open flame because alcohol vapor burns.

2. Collect some alcohol in a container. Then turn off the heat. When the cooker is cool, open it. Dispose of the remaining liquid. Only then is it safe to test whether the collected alcohol will burn. Wrap a bit of cotton on a stick and moisten it with the distilled liquid. Ignite and observe how alcohol looks as it burns.

3. Carry out the activity in a well-ventilated place.

4. It is not a good idea to taste the alcohol. Because of the crude fermentation procedure, it will contain contaminants that often produce nausea and vomiting.

Evaluation: depends upon which activities are pursued; in general, participation in each activity used

ACTIVITY TWELVE:

Cultivating Nonflowering Plants: Algae

Objective: to learn about and grow algae

Materials: clumps of algae

containers

two goldfish tanks

one or two goldfish

Procedure: Begin by communicating the following information to your class. In the plant kingdom, the most noticeable phyla is that of the flowering plants. These include trees, shrubs, grasses, and leafy plants. There is a group of plants that have no flowers. Some produce new plants from spores and include mosses, ferns, fungi, and algae. The life cycle of these plants is different from that of flowering plants. Since they don't produce seed, propagation is usually done from spores or from parts of the plant.

Algae, a single-celled plant that usually grows in long filaments, is easy to propagate. Clumps of algae can be broken apart by your students and small bits should be started in new containers. People who study food growth processes have been interested in the relationship between plant-eating fish and algae. Common goldfish exhibit this relationship with algae. If two similar tanks are filled with water and inoculated with some shredded algae, an interesting experiment can be conducted. The only difference between the two tanks is that one or two goldfish are added to one of the tanks. Nothing more is added except a bit of water to replace the water that evaporates. Both tanks should be kept in a well-lighted place where they get a few hours of sun each day. Students should keep records for a month in the form shown in Figure 3.9.

Children will discover that the plant-animal tank shows a clearly different weight gain when compared with the tank with the algae alone.

Evaluation: successful completion of activities as directed, including the record described

FIGURE 3.9
Algae record form

TANK 1 Water and algae	TANK 2 Water, algae, and goldfish
Weight of algae added to tank _____	Weight of algae and goldfish added to tank _____
After one month	
New weight of algae in tank _____	New weight of algae and goldfish in tank _____

ACTIVITY THIRTEEN:

Nonflowering Plants: Moss

Objective: to grow and learn about moss as a nonflowering plant

Materials: clumps of moss

cups of soil

flats

cheesecloth

plastic

Procedure: Moss can be grown from pieces of moss found in the garden or woods. Moss is often found in moist, shady places, growing on rocks or soil made up of decaying plant matter. Have your class prepare a flat with soil that is acidic. Soil can be acidified in several ways, although soil that is composed of humus or compost is usually acidic. An easy way to acidify soil is to add about one tablespoon full of powdered milk per pound of soil.

Have groups of students select a small clump of moss that has a slightly dried-out appearance and examine it carefully. They should find small, brown, spearlike projections on the top of the green moss shoots. This is the spore container. Instruct the groups to allow the moss to dry a bit and then pulverize it by rubbing it between their hands.

Have students remove a cup of soil from the top of their flats and mix this with the pulverized moss. They should smooth the soil in the flat and lay a single layer of cheesecloth over the flat. Next, have them sprinkle the moss-soil mixture over the cheesecloth and pat it gently. Instruct them that the flat must be kept moist, cool, and out of direct sunlight. They should keep the flat covered with plastic and allow 6 weeks for a good layer of moss to form on the cheesecloth. The cheesecloth is used because it makes it possible to lift the moss from the flat. The moss can be used as a soil cover in a flowerpot or in an ornamental dish arrangement. It also makes a fine ground cover for a woodland terrarium.

Evaluation: successful growing of moss, individually or through active small-group participation

ACTIVITY FOURTEEN:

Forced Bulbs

Objective: to force bulbs to flower

Materials: variety of bulbs

mesh container

deep containers filled with sand or gravel and soil

humus or ground moss

pans for water

Procedure: Late in the fall, nurseries often sell remaining bulbs at reduced prices. This is the time to purchase bulbs for forcing. Forcing is the name of the process used to encourage bulbs to bloom at almost any time of the year. After purchase, store bulbs in a mesh container in a cool place. They can be kept on a shelf in the refrigerator. Since it takes about 6 weeks to bring a bulb to bloom, time the forcing procedure so you will have blossoms when you want them.

To force bulbs, first help students select containers having depths of about six times the diameter of the bulbs. Have them place one or two inches of clean sand or fine gravel in the bottom of the container, then add an inch of rich, sandy soil. The students can prepare the soil by mixing one part sand with one part humus or ground peat moss. Students should arrange several bulbs on this layer and cover the bulbs with more soil. They should then cover the bulbs to a depth of three or four times the diameter of the bulb.

The pots should next be set in pans of water for thirty minutes, then taken out and drained. Students should place the pots in a cool, dark, ventilated place for some time, the exact length of which depends on how quickly individual bulbs sprout (usually four to six weeks). Students should check the pots weekly for signs of life. As soon as they see the soil begin to crack and plant tips appear, or at the end of six weeks, they should place the pots on a warm, well-lighted windowsill. Many bulbs, including tulips, hyacinths, daffodils, and crocus, are suitable for forcing.

Evaluation: successful flowering of forced bulbs

UNIT EVALUATION: RADIO BROADCAST OR VIDEO

Have students work in teams of three or four. Have each team prepare a 3- to 5-minute radio broadcast or video about the five key things they learned during this unit. The radio broadcast or video could be shared with other classes or parents. This evaluation activity could be used with any unit.

ADDITIONAL ACTIVITIES:

Extension and/or Evaluation

1. Using a variety of seeds, have students make mosaics. They each should choose a subject, draw or outline their picture, then fill it in by gluing seeds to the paper. This project can be given an historical perspective by discussing the mosaics of such ancient civilizations as Greece and Rome.

2. Instead of relying solely on seeds, start new plants from vegetables. Sections of potatoes, carrots, and pineapples as well as avocado pits can be placed in containers filled with water, sand, or vermiculite to produce new plants. Start several at once and compare their rates of growth.

3. Many tasty activities can be pursued using seeds as the main or only ingredients. Cook with, or simply taste and compare, such items as peanuts, sunflower seeds, peas, baked beans, sesame seeds, and coconuts. Or explore the seeds and pits found in fruits. Cherries, grapes, peaches, apples, and oranges are delicious sources of easy-to-find, yet varied, seeds.

4. Help students create art objects from edible fruits and vegetables. Use toothpicks to combine various sized and shaped pieces of fruits and vegetables into sculptures. Encourage the students to taste bits of the various foods as they create the shapes desired for their final products. Or let them try their hands at carving stamps from potatoes, and then creating stamped pictures and designs.

5. Have students explore the effect of climate and environment on plant life. They can create maps showing the locations of various types of vegetation throughout the world.

Students can also learn from the selections of state trees and flowers. Have them plot these on a U.S. map, then look for patterns and similarities in various regions of the country. Have students speculate as to the reasons for states' choices.

6. Students can create lovely pictures by making leaf rubbings. Leaves are positioned under a piece of paper, then various shades of crayons are rubbed over the paper, creating on the paper the image of the leaf underneath. The beauty of autumn leaves can also be preserved by sealing them between sheets of waxed paper.

7. This theme contains numerous opportunities to involve students in measurement activities. A bit of reflection will indicate that children have made judgments about weight, volume, length, temperature, and area. This can be a very effective way to introduce or sustain the concept of measurement by embedding the concept in a series of activities that have something else (i.e., growing) as their primary focal point.

8. Have students check your software collection, media center, or the Internet for additional information about plants. Prepare a list of resources for the class.

Teacher Resources

See Appendix B for resources and addresses.

ENVIRONMENTS

Environments: Land use and climatic influences on life-styles, along with map reading and map making, are included in this theme. Logical inferences are encouraged by examining actual maps made of the same area several years apart. Implications are discussed.

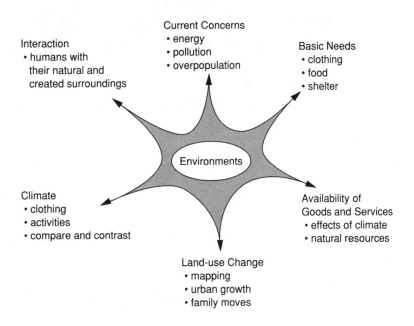

Interaction
• humans with
  their natural and
  created surroundings

Current Concerns
• energy
• pollution
• overpopulation

Basic Needs
• clothing
• food
• shelter

Environments

Climate
• clothing
• activities
• compare and contrast

Availability of
Goods and Services
• effects of climate
• natural resources

Land-use Change
• mapping
• urban growth
• family moves

INTRODUCTION

Since time began, the human race has been preoccupied with adaptation to its environment. In the early years this struggle was much less complex than it is today. Then, the search for food, clothing, and shelter occupied most of people's time and effort. Today, the interaction between an individual and the environment involves many other variables. For example, the issues of availability of energy, pollution, and world overpopulation reflect the complexity of the continuing struggle for adaptation to the environment.

This theme is of necessity restricted to a much smaller scale. It deals with the issue of children adapting to their environments. They are placed in situations designed to emphasize the impact that various aspects of the environment (climate, land use, availability of goods and services) have upon their daily lives. Activities stress group participation as well as individual interactions. This theme enables children to compare and reflect on the differences and similarities between the old and the new. Valuable insights into human nature can result from such reflection.

Unit Objectives. Students will:

1. develop an awareness of the effects of climate on human life.
2. compare and contrast climates and make inferences about life in those climates.
3. recognize land-use changes and factors that influence them.
4. improve skills in reading and drawing maps.
5. learn how to construct, conduct, and evaluate the results of surveys.

Appropriate Grade Levels. Elementary and Middle School

Vocabulary.

climate	population
weather	pollution
land-use	season
urban	survey
rural	cultural features
natural resources	

Note: See Appendix A for planning sheets.

ACTIVITY ONE:

Climate 1

Objective:	to rank items on an activity sheet and participate in a decision-making activity
Materials:	pencils
	reproduced Activity Sheet 1 or Seasonal Items Sheet (Figure 3.10)
Procedure:	Read the following hypothetical situation to the class.

After living in Minnesota for seven years, your family has moved to California. Mark, a friend who now lives next door, is going to Minnesota to visit his grandfather and

FIGURE 3.10

Seasonal items sheet

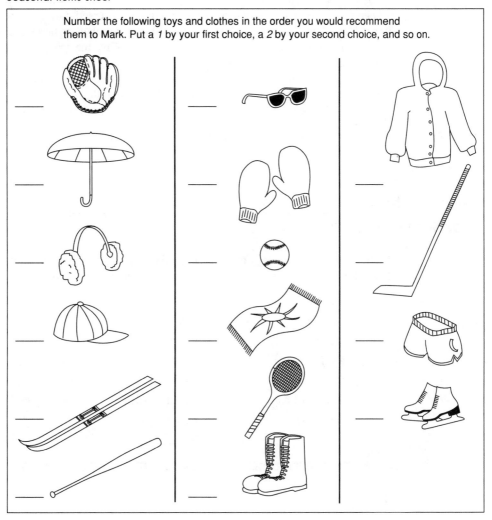

grandmother. This will be his first visit and he is going during the wintertime. Mark has asked you and your brothers and sisters what he should take with him.

Note: Other states of similar climates can be substituted for those used in order to make the situation more directly related to your students' experiences.

After reading the scenario, pass out either Sheet 1 or the Seasonal Items Sheet in Figure 3.10 to each child. Ask children to number the items in the order they would recommend them to Mark: a *1* by their first choice, a *2* by their second choice, and so on. If someone in the class is new to your area, the sheet can be marked based on what he or she thinks the weather might be like during the winter.

After everyone has completed the sheet, put the children together in "family" groups of four or five. Then tell the class, "Mark has asked you and your brothers and sisters to recommend some clothes and toys to take with him. Now you must decide as a group what things you would suggest to him. You should have just one list when you are finished."

Have each group choose a recorder or appoint one yourself. Give each recorder an additional worksheet. Tell the children that they should not change the numbers on their own sheet even if the group list is not the same as theirs. Give the groups as much time as you feel is necessary for completion of this task.

Ask each recorder to read, in order, the list the group decided on. When the lists are shared, ask the children how they knew which things might be useful to Mark. Finally, ask how the choices would be different if Mark were going to Minnesota in the summer.

Evaluation: completion of activity sheet individually, and active participation in group rankings and discussions

---

Activity Sheet 1

SEASONAL SUGGESTIONS

Number the following toys and clothes in the order you would recommend them to Mark. Put a *1* by your first choice, a *2* by your second choice, and so on.

____ a baseball glove	____ a ball
____ an umbrella	____ a beach towel
____ earmuffs	____ a tennis racket
____ a cap	____ boots
____ skis	____ a lined jacket
____ a baseball bat	____ a hockey stick
____ sunglasses	____ a bathing suit
____ mittens	____ ice skates

ACTIVITY TWO:

Climate 2

Objective: to conduct a survey of an adult and a teenager, to tally and summarize the results, and to hypothesize about how the results might change

Materials: three Survey Sheets for each student

pencils

Procedure: Ask the class to recall some of the items on the sheet from Activity One. Ask whether there are items that they use mainly in either the summer or winter, or whether they use the same items throughout the year.

Then ask the class how they could find out what activities other people like to do in the summer and winter, or throughout the year if their climate has little seasonal change. After discussing how they might keep a record of their answers, suggest that each child survey two other people, if possible one teenager and one adult. Each of those surveyed should record their choices on a survey sheet. You may choose to use Activity Sheet 2 or, if the items on the sheet are inappropriate because of your climate, have the children make up their own Survey Sheet. The survey should be conducted after school so that the results can be discussed prior to the next lesson. Each child in the class should also fill out a Survey Sheet.

Discuss the results of the survey prior to Activity Three. To begin the discussion, draw a large Survey Sheet on the board where the children can record their responses. The results can be tallied either by having the children record their responses during free time or by asking them to come up individually and mark their responses at the start of the discussion.

Now discuss the results of the survey.

1. What activity do most of the adults like to do in the summer? In the winter?
2. What activity do most teenagers like to do in the summer? In the winter?
3. What activity do most of the children like to do in the summer? In the winter?
4. How might these results change if more people were surveyed?

Evaluation: completion of survey as directed, and participation in group discussion of the survey results

---

Activity Sheet 2
SURVEY SHEET

Please check whether you are a child, a teenager, or an adult. Then put a check by your favorite activity in the summer and in the winter.

Child _____ Teenager _____ Adult _____

In the summer the outdoor activity I like best is:

Swimming _____	Baseball _____
Biking _____	Golfing _____
Camping _____	Tennis _____
Gardening _____	Fishing _____
Line skating _____	Other _____
Walking _____	

In the winter the outdoor activity I like best is:

Skiing _____	Ice fishing _____
Skating _____	Hockey _____
Sledding _____	Playing in the snow _____
Snowshoeing _____	Other _____
Tobogganing _____	

ACTIVITY THREE:

Comparing Climates

Objective: to make inferences about the climates of two cities and to compare and contrast these two climates

Materials: Yellow Pages Worksheets (Figures 3.11 and 3.12)

transparency

pencils

reproduced Activity Sheet 3

United States map for each child

YELLOW PAGES FOR CITY A

Air Conditioning Equipment

JOE'S AIR CONDITIONERS

HAS ALL BRANDS

Garden Stores

CACTUSLAND

WE SELL CACTUS AND PALM TREES

Awnings

COOL-RAY AWNINGS

KEEP YOUR HOME COOL!

Sporting Goods

Speedway Sports
WE SELL SPORTING GOODS FOR
**FISHING GOLF
BASEBALL & TENNIS**

Camping Equipment

THE BACKPACKER

WE SELL TENTS, SLEEPING BAGS, AND BACKPACKS

Swimming Pools

WILSON POOLS

WE BUILD POOLS ALL YEAR LONG!
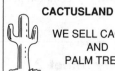

Furnaces

DAY & NIGHT FURNACES

WE'VE SOLD FURNACES FOR **50** YEARS

Garden and Lawn Sprinklers

LATHAM SPRINKLERS

WE INSTALL AUTOMATIC OR MANUAL SYSTEMS

FIGURE 3.11
Yellow pages worksheet, city A

YELLOW PAGES FOR CITY B

Air Conditioning
Equipment

WE SELL
AIR CONDITIONERS
FOR A ROOM OR
A WHOLE HOUSE

Skating Equipment

SILVER SKATE SHOP
We Sell New
and Used
Skates

Awnings

AWNINGS, INC.

Snow Removal Services

PLOW ·YOU· OUT

DRIVEWAYS AND
PARKING LOTS
CLEARED

Camping Equipment

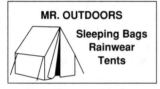

MR. OUTDOORS

Sleeping Bags
Rainwear
Tents

Snow Vehicles

SNOW KING

WE HAVE **6** KINDS OF
SNOWMOBILES

Furnaces

ACE HEATING COMPANY

LET US HELP YOU
KEEP YOUR HOUSE
WARM THIS WINTER!

Sporting Goods

MIKE'S
SPORTING GOODS
We Have Clothes for
Hockey, Skiing, Golf,
Tennis, and Baseball

Garden Stores

WE SELL <u>EVERYTHING</u>
FOR YOUR YARD!

Swimming Pools

P👀L FUN

TOYS
PARTS

FIGURE 3.12
Yellow pages worksheet, city B

City A	Both Cities A & B	City B

FIGURE 3.13
Comparison diagram: cities A and B

Procedure: Ask the children, "How is your house or apartment adapted to the climate in which you live? Would there be a difference if your home were located in another climate?" Then ask, "What are some sports that depend upon a certain kind of climate? Are there some sports that can't be played where we live?"

After discussing these questions, pass out to each student a copy of both Yellow Pages worksheets. These can be worked on individually or in pairs. Then pass out a copy of Activity Sheet 3 to each child. Ask the class to look through the Yellow Pages Worksheet for City A. From the goods and services listed, they should mark on the activity sheet the kinds of weather they think City A has and a word or picture that helped them determine this. Then have the class look at the Yellow Pages Worksheet for City B and follow the same procedure used for City A.

When Activity Sheet 3 has been completed by each student, make a diagram like Figure 3.13 to compare the two cities. Ask the class the following questions:

1. What goods and services did both cities have? Which ones did one city have that the other did not?

2. What inferences can you make about City A's climate? City B's?

Now pass out a copy of a United States map to each student. Ask students in what areas of the country City A and City B might be located. Have them give reasons for their answers. After everyone has had a chance to respond, point out the location of City A (Tucson, Arizona) and City B (Saint Paul, Minnesota). Finish by comparing students' answers with the correct information and discussing any differences or similarities between the two. You might wish to set up a chart or graph to analyze the various answers given by the class.

Evaluation: completion of Activity Sheet 3 and participation in group discussions

Activity Sheet 3
CLIMATE

Look at the goods and services advertised for City A. Put a check by each of the kinds of weather you think that city might have. On the line, put the word or picture shown in the ad that helped you decide. Then do the same for City B.

City A's Climate	*City B's Climate*
Wet _____	Wet _____
Dry _____	Dry _____
Snowy _____	Snowy _____
Sunny _____	Sunny _____
Cloudy _____	Cloudy _____
Hot _____	Hot _____
Cold _____	Cold _____
Windy _____	Windy _____

ACTIVITY FOUR:
Land-Use Change

Objective: to make inferences about land-use change after listening to a story and to hypothesize about environmental changes that may take place during the next fifty years

Materials: the book *The Little House* by Virginia Lee Burton

Procedure: Before reading the book, ask the class to list some of the things that are around them (e.g., desks and chairs). Then ask them to name items that would be around them if they went outdoors (e.g., trees, grass, or snow). Ask whether anyone knows the word for what surrounds a person. Whether a student knows or you tell them, print the word *environment* on the board. Then tell the class that you are going to read a story about a little house. They should listen carefully for the different kinds of environments in which the little house was found.

Read *The Little House* to the class. As you read, show as many of the pictures as possible. After you have finished the story, ask the following questions:

1. Which part of the little house's environment stayed the same for many years?

2. Which part of its environment changed?

3. What kinds of things did the city add as it grew larger?

4. Why do you think the city grew?

5. Did the changes happen over a short or a long period of time? How do you know?

6. Why do you think no one wanted to live in the little house once other buildings were all around it? Would you have lived in it?

7. Think about the city in this story. How do you think your community looked 50 years ago?

Then ask the children what their environment might be like 50 years from now. Which parts of their environment will probably be the same as they are now? Which parts could change? Continue the discussion as long as the children seem interested and involved.

Evaluation: active participation in class discussion

ACTIVITY FIVE:

Maps and Land-Use Change

Objective: to hypothesize about the meanings of map symbols and, after looking at two maps, to hypothesize about the ages and areas represented by each

Materials: chalkboard and chalk

copies for each child of two maps showing land-use change

Procedure: Remind the class that *The Little House* talked about land-use change. Tell them that geographers can study changes in the land by looking at photographs taken from an airplane. They can make a map from a photograph and then compare maps of the same area made from photographs taken a few years apart.

Tell the children that they are now going to look at two maps that have been drawn from airplane photographs. Explain that geographers use symbols for the features of the photographs and put these symbols on their maps. Put these symbols on the chalkboard and ask the class what features these symbols might stand for. After students have given their ideas, tell them the correct answers. Geographers' symbols and the names of what they represent are shown on the Student Map Sheets in Figures 3.14 and 3.15.

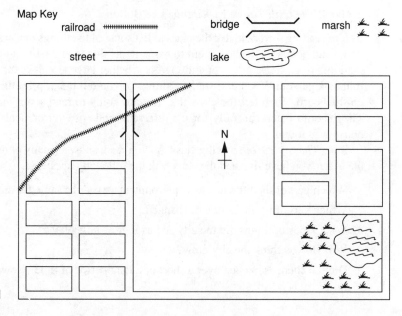

FIGURE 3.14
Student map sheet 1

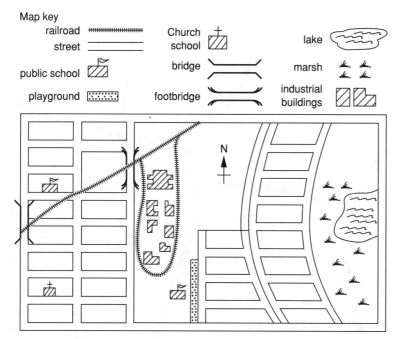

Map key
railroad ╫╫╫╫╫╫╫╫╫╫
street ═══════
public school
playground
Church
school
bridge
footbridge
lake
marsh
industrial
buildings

FIGURE 3.15
Student map sheet 2: 30 years
later

After the discussion and symbol identification, which can be done independently or in small groups, pass out copies of Student Map Sheet 1 and Student Map Sheet 2: 30 Years Later. Ask the children to study the two maps and look for some of the symbols that were discussed earlier. The map key will help them. After the children have had sufficient time to study the maps, ask the following questions:

1. What are some of the things you found on the maps?

2. Could these be maps of the same area? Why or why not?

3. After the children have come to the conclusion that they could be maps of the same area, tell them that in fact they are. Ask, which maps is older? How can you tell?

4. What might have caused the changes that you see in the newer map?

This same activity could be done using an area in your community. Draw a map showing the area 30 years ago and another showing the same area today. Have students discuss symbols and land-use change. You could make slides of some of the features and have students match the pictures with the symbols on the newer map.

Evaluation: participation in discussions, with answers indicating an understanding of the symbols and concepts presented

ACTIVITY SIX:

Planning Land-Use

Objective: to complete a map of New City using the symbols presented in Activity Five and to compare this with the actual map

FIGURE 3.16
Student map of New City

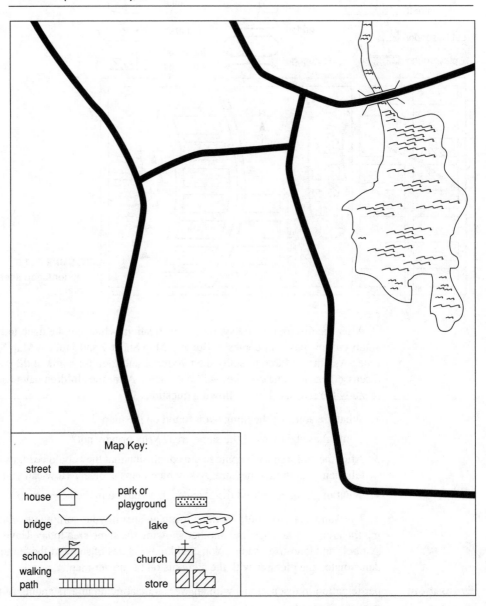

Materials: Student map of New City for each student (Figure 3.16)

Actual map of New City made into a transparency (Figure 3.17)

pencils

overhead projector

FIGURE 3.17

Actual map of New City

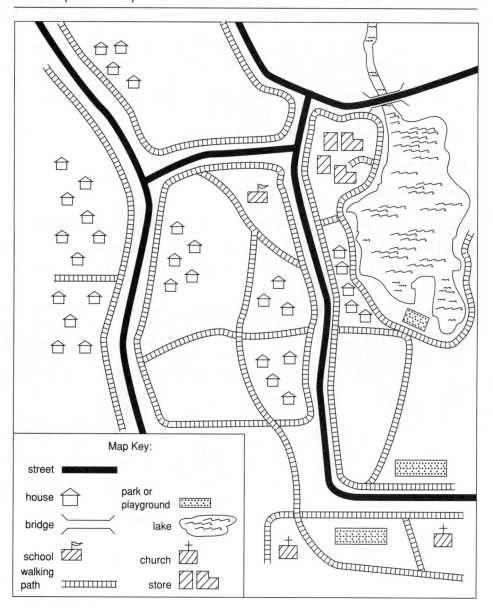

Map Key:

street

house   park or
                playground

bridge   lake

school   church
walking
path   store

Procedure: Pass out a Student Map of New City to each child. Tell the class that this is a map of a city
that is just being built, and that it is being built on farmland. Review the use of symbols and
what these symbols stand for.

Then ask the children to fill in the rest of the map of New City, putting in houses, walking paths, churches, stores, and parks. Have them put these things wherever they think they

should be located. Remind them to use the map key for their symbols. As the children are working on their maps, walk around and ask each child the reasons for his or her choices. If you are unable to talk to each child, try to see those you missed after the lesson has been completed.

When the children have finished their maps, show them a transparency of where things are actually located in New City. Ask how their choices were the same and how they were different. Ask the class what the advantages are of building a city on land where there are only a few houses. What might be some of the disadvantages? How many of them would like to live in New City? Use Figure 3.13.

Evaluation: completion of a New City map by each student

ACTIVITY SEVEN:

Role-Playing Skills

Objective: to participate in a role-playing situation about a family move decision

Materials: New City Information Sheet (Figure 3.18) for each student

role-playing slip (cut from Activity Sheet 7) for each family member (one set of cards for each small group)

Procedure: Tell the students that in today's activity they are going to pretend to be someone else. Assign each person to be either a mother, father, 16-year-old brother, 10-year-old brother, or 7-year-old sister. After each child has a family role, place students in groups of five that have one of each of the above-named members. The children should be seated so that it will be easy for them to communicate with the other members of their "family."

COME TO NEW CITY!

THERE ARE PLACES TO WALK, FISH, SAIL, HORSEBACK RIDE, AND PLAY.

THERE ARE WALKING PATHS TO EVERY PLACE IN NEW CITY.

THE LAND HAS BEAUTIFUL HOUSES AND LAKES, WOODS, AND PARKS.

THERE ARE MANY KINDS OF HOUSES AT MANY DIFFERENT PRICES. THERE ARE HOUSES TO BUY AND HOUSES TO RENT.

CLOSE TO YOUR HOME WILL BE A PLACE TO SHOP.

FIGURE 3.18
New City information sheet

THERE ARE LOTS OF JOBS AND THERE WILL BE MORE IN THE NEXT FEW YEARS.

Tell the class, "Yesterday you learned a little bit about a city called New City. Today's lessons will also be about this city." Pass out a New City Information Sheet to each group and have one child in each group read it aloud to the other members.

Next, say, "Your family is thinking about moving to New City from where you now live. Some of your family members would like to move and others aren't sure. Here is the way the person you are pretending to be feels." Give each family member a role slip. Continue by saying, "Read your role sheet. Your family is going to discuss moving to New City and this sheet will help you in the discussion." Give the children time to read their sheets and ask any questions they have about their roles.

Ask one of the "parents" to start the discussion, then the others should join in, telling how they feel about moving to New City. Tell students that at the end of the discussion (10 minutes) they should decide as a family whether to move or stay where they live now. After the discussions, ask each "father" or "mother" what the family's decision is. If there is time, you can form a new set of families and have students role-play different members of the family.

Evaluation: participation by each child in a role-playing group

---

Activity Sheet 7
ROLE-PLAYING SLIPS

Cut the slips apart on the dotted lines and give one slip to each "family" member.

Mother   You like the neighborhood you live in now. Almost every morning, you take your children's grandmother shopping, to the doctor, or out for a drive. In the afternoon you work at the school near your house. You have just heard about a good, full-time job nearby that you may be interested in.

Father   If you moved to New City, you are sure you could get a job in the Canning Company. Then, it would take you only 5 minutes to drive to work and maybe you could walk. Now it takes you an hour to drive to work. You could fish in the lake at New City during your time off.

Older Brother   You are a junior in high school and have a lot of friends. You're not sure you would see them very often if you moved so far away. You like to go to movies and to bowl. The closest theaters and bowling alleys to New City are in another town 15 minutes away.

Younger Brother   You are in fifth grade and like to be outdoors all the time. Every weekend you go fishing with a friend or with your father. You'd like to move to New City because you could go horseback riding as well as fish.

Sister   You are in third grade. You have a very good friend who lives next door to you. You like to be outdoors after school. When you drove to New City, you saw lots of children who looked your age. You also saw some houses that you'd like to live in.

ACTIVITY EIGHT:

Land-Use Change

Objective: to describe land-use around your school and to construct a map showing suggested land-use changes

Materials: drawing paper

crayons and pencils

Procedure: Discuss with the class how the land around their school is being used. If possible, take a walk around the area after raising the question, and continue the discussion after returning.

Ask whether anyone knows of changes in the area that have recently taken place, and whether they know the reasons for the changes. If not, ask some children to try to find out. If some of the children do not live in the school's neighborhood, ask them how the land around their homes is being used and whether there have been any recent changes.

Pass out a piece of drawing paper to each of the children. Ask them to think about some changes they would like to make in the use of the land in their own neighborhood, and then to draw a picture showing how the land would look after their changes. Some of the children might wish to make an aerial map of the changes. These children can use symbols for the features in their maps.

When the maps or pictures are completed, put all of the drawings and maps on a bulletin board with the reasons for the land-use changes beside each picture. Be careful to praise students for the creativity of their suggestions rather than for the drawing itself.

Evaluation: completion of land-use change picture or map

UNIT EVALUATION: LITTLE BOOK

Have students work individually to make little books that summarize what they have learned about the environment. Directions for making a little book are provided in Figure 3.19.

1. Fold a sheet of paper to make 8 squares.

2. Fold paper in half on the solid line. Cut to the first fold.

3. Open the sheet and fold along the long fold. Push both ends together.

4. Fold the sides to complete the little book.

1	8	7	6
2	3	4	5

FIGURE 3.19
Making a little book

ADDITIONAL ACTIVITIES:

Extension and Evaluation

1. Examine with your students how your community has changed in the past 30 years. Then have students predict how it might change in the next year and 30 years in the future.

2. Help your students to directly affect their school or community environment. Engage them in an active program to clean up litter, plant flowers or saplings, or otherwise enhance the inside or outside appearance of their school building. Your students could also measure the attitudes of their fellow students by surveying their feelings about the appearance of their school building and grounds before and after changes have been made.

3. Have students continue to explore the environment using the Greenhaven Press Opposing Viewpoints Juniors Series (*The Environment, Animal Rights, Endangered Species, Forests, Garbage, Nuclear Power, Pollution, Population, Toxic Wastes,* and *Zoos*), Greenhaven Press, Inc., PO Box 289009, San Diego, CA 92198. 1-800-231-5163.

4. Select additional activities related to the environment from the following resources:
   Earth Book for Kids by Linda Schwartz. Santa Barbara, CA: Learning Works, 1990.
   Going Green: A Kid's Handbook to Saving the Planet by John Elkington, Douglas Hill, and Julia Hailes. New York: Viking, 1990.
   I Can Save the Earth: A Kid's Handbook for Keeping the Earth Healthy and Green by Anita Holmes. New York: Messner, 1993.
   Save the Earth: An Action Handbook for Kids by Betty Miles. New York: Knopf, 1991.
   Take Action: An Environmental Book for Kids by Anne Love and Jane Drake. New York: Beech Tree, 1992.
   Teaching Kids to Love the Earth by Marina Herman, Joseph Passineau, Ann Schimpf, and Paul Trever. Duluth, MN: Pfeiffer Hamilton, 1991.

5. Create a classroom display of books about the environment that could include the following:
   The Changing Earth by Dougal Dixon. New York: Thompson Learning, 1993.
   Protecting the Planet by Colin Harris. New York: Thompson Learning, 1993.
   Natural Resources by Damian Randle. New York: Thompson Learning, 1993.
   The Super Science Book of the Environment by Sally Morgan. New York: Thompson, 1994.

Teacher Resources

Counting on People, ZPG Population Education Program. 1400 16th St NW, Suite 320, Washington, DC 20036.

Environmental Issues by Pauline Chandler. Huntington Beach, CA: Teacher-Created Materials. 1994.

50 Simple Things You Can Do to Save the Earth by the Earth Works Group. Kansas City, MO: Andrews & McMeel, 1990.

The Environment: Using Nonfiction to Promote Literacy Across the Curriculum. Columbus, OH: Fearon Press, 1993.

Global Alert! Understanding the Environmental Problems Facing Our Planet. Columbus, OH: Good Apple, 1992.

See Appendix B for additional resources and addresses.

ENERGY

Energy: These activities emphasize measurement of energy consumption, methods of energy conservation, and related data-collection techniques. Heat, solar, mechanical, and electrical energy are considered.

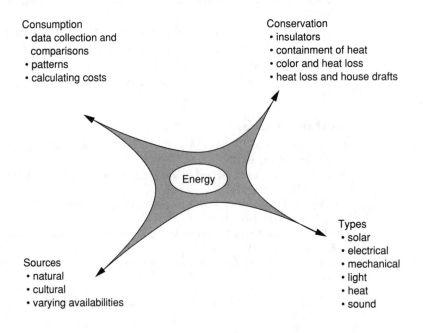

Consumption
• data collection and
  comparisons
• patterns
• calculating costs

Conservation
• insulators
• containment of heat
• color and heat loss
• heat loss and house drafts

Energy

Sources
• natural
• cultural
• varying availabilities

Types
• solar
• electrical
• mechanical
• light
• heat
• sound

INTRODUCTION

Energy has profound effects on many aspects of our economy as well as on our environment. Some of these effects are positive in nature: for example, expanded use of smaller, more economical automobiles, renewed efforts to locate and develop additional sources of energy, and the evolution of a more energy-conscious citizenry.

Classroom teachers throughout the nation can encourage students to discuss and research various ramifications of wise use of energy and begin to detail the implications for all of us. Mathematics can provide an added dimension to such activities, for only through a quantitative analysis of energy use can one begin to understand both the implications of a shortage and the magnitude of the energy-reducing measures required to counteract one.

For example, school children can be asked to determine the level of energy consumption in their own homes. Such an activity will also provide valuable experience with the collection and manipulation of gathered data.

For comparison purposes, it is necessary for students to have access to baseline data. Local electrical power and natural gas companies regularly compile data on the amounts of gas and electricity used and the costs to the consumer. The companies will supply this data to interested persons on request. Energy usage is a function of climate and thus varies from place to place.

Many activities can result from classroom energy-related discussions and subsequent analysis of data collected. The variety of activities is limited only by the originality of the students and teachers involved.

The ultimate benefit in such activities lies not in getting the right answer but in sensitizing students to the implications that a major national crisis might have for a concerned citizenry. In addition, these activities provide meaningful opportunities to use basic skills and mathematical techniques. Students will be using data-collection techniques, sampling and estimative procedures, and analytic techniques in a manner that is both useful and significant.

An important component of these lessons is the student discussion that should follow the actual activities. Whenever possible, encourage students to deal with the social aspects of energy consumption. Emphasize the role and responsibility of each individual and household in dealing realistically with our nation's energy resources.

Remember that the specific individual activities in and of themselves are less important than the total concept that the child will develop. You should be more concerned that children develop an energy consciousness than with the mastery of any particular subconcept.

Unit Objectives. Students will:

1. learn techniques related to surveying, measuring, and recording energy consumption.

2. examine ways to use energy wisely.

3. be able to calculate the costs of energy consumption and the savings of conserving energy.

4. create a display of what they have learned and what they recommend about energy.

5. learn about various kinds and sources of energy, and produce some kinds of energy themselves (e.g., electrical or solar).

Appropriate Grade Levels. Elementary and Middle School

Vocabulary.

energy   insulator   consumption

solar   conservation   containment

Note: See Appendix A for planning sheets.

ACTIVITY ONE:

Individual Surveys

Objective: to complete individual home energy use surveys and share these surveys with the class

TABLE 3.2
Annual use of electricity

Annual Use of Electricity in Kilowatt Hours (A 100-watt bulb burning 10 hours equals 1 kilowatt hour)
Annual Northern States Power Output—25,059,000,000 Kilowatt Hours. * *Percentages Used by Various Customers:*

Residences	.32.8
Small commercial and industrial	.14.1
Large commercial and industrial	.42.1
Street lighting and others	3.2
Municipalities	3.6
Rural electrical cooperative	0.3
Other electric companies	3.9

Average Annual Use of Electricity by One Residence—7,049 Kilowatt Hours
Average Annual Use of Electricity, Expressed in Kilowatt Hours, by Various Appliances:

Clock Radio	96
Coffee maker (used twice a day)	96
Washing machine (used 12 hours a month)	108
VCR	225
Dishwasher	360
Black-and-white television	600
Conventional refrigerator	796
Clothes dryer (used 16 hours a month)	960
Computer	1,000
Range (for family of 4)	.1,200
Color television	.1,200
Frostless refrigerator-freezer	.2,000

*Lighting a home in wintertime figures out to about 10 kilowatt hours per month a room (50 for a five-room house); in the summer, with longer daylight hours, the use of electricity for lighting would be less.

Figures from the Northern States Power Company; appliance figures based on average use of electricity in the Twin Cities metropolitan area.

Materials:	paper and pencils
Procedure:	Ask individual students to survey the energy consumption of their own homes. They should be able to note the kind of energy as well as the amount consumed. Students should agree upon a form for recording the results of their surveys.
	Once surveys are completed, make a class graph of the average yearly, monthly, or weekly levels of energy consumption. Use group data to determine whether levels of consumption are less than, equal to, or greater than large-group averages quoted in tables. Discuss practical methods of curtailing energy consumption.
Evaluation:	successful completion of both individual surveys and the class graph

ACTIVITY TWO:

Annual Energy Consumption

Objective:	to measure annual energy consumption, and to construct problems relative to that consumption
Materials:	paper and pencils
	Tables 3.2, 3.3, 3.4, and 3.5

TABLE 3.3
Annual use of gas

Total Annual Distribution of Gas by Minnegasco in Minneapolis and Suburbs (Including all of Hennepin County and Parts of Wright, Anoka, and Dakota Counties)—107 Billion Cubic Feet*

Percentages of Output Used by Various Customers:

Residences using gas for heating	.43
Commercial establishments using gas, including heating	.14
Commercial establishments using gas, but not for heating	1
Industrial use of gas, including heating	2
Industrial use of gas, but not for heating	1
Part time industrial and commercial (interruptable)	.39

The percentage figures are rounded out; use of gas by residences that do not heat by gas accounts for a fractional use too small to be taken into account.

Cubic Feet

Average annual use of gas for heating by one residence (three-bedroom rambler)	147,000
Average annual use of gas in one residence for water heating	29,000
Average annual use of gas in one residence for cooking	14,000
Average annual use of gas in one residence for drying clothes	5,500
Average annual use of gas by one yard light (figured at 2 cubic feet an hour over 365 days)	17,520

*Figures, but not percentages, from Minnegasco.

TABLE 3.4
Cost to the consumer

Per Kilowatt—Cost of Residential Electricity Consumed	
	Rate
October Through May	6.03 cents per kilowatt hour (kwh)
June to September	6.83 cents per kilowatt hour (kwh)

TABLE 3.5
Natural gas rates for residential and commercial consumption

Cost of Residential and Commercial Natural Gas Consumed	
	Rate
	43.91 cents per 100 cubic feet

Procedure: Before pursuing this activity, you will need to consult appropriate tables of data. You may use the tables that are included with this activity, or obtain your own from your local library or energy companies.

Once data have been obtained, ask students to use those data to find the answers to the following questions:

1. How many kilowatt hours of electricity are consumed annually by:
   a. residences?
   b. small commercial and industrial companies?
2. How many cubic feet of natural gas are consumed annually by:
   a. residences using gas for heating?
   b. commercial establishments?

These are just examples of the kinds of questions you can present to your students. Once questions have been answered and students have become comfortable with the tables, have them make up problems that can be answered by using the tables and exchange these with other students for solving.

Evaluation: correct answers given for questions posed, and completion of student-constructed problems

ACTIVITY THREE:

Energy Survey

Objective: to conduct an energy consumption survey

Materials: paper and pencils, or Home Energy Cost Survey Sheet (Figure 3.20) and Table 3.6

Procedure: Have class members conduct an energy consumption survey of their homes. Ask them to use Table 3.6 and Figure 3.20 to calculate the cost of next month's electric bill. Have each

FIGURE 3.20
Home energy cost survey sheet

CHECK THOSE APPLIANCES FOUND IN YOUR HOME

Yes	No	Appliance	Average Annual Kilowatt Hours Used	My House	Monthly Cost
___	___	Vacuum cleaner	48	_____	_____
___	___	Clock Radio	96	_____	_____
___	___	Coffee maker	96	_____	_____
___	___	Frostless refrigerator-freezer	2,004	_____	_____
___	___	Other (i.e., electrical lights)	_____	_____	_____
		Totals	_____	_____	_____

1. Is your total electrical consumption higher or lower than the average?
_____ Higher   _____ Lower
2. By how much? _____
3. How could energy consumption in your home be reduced?
_____

TABLE 3.6
Home appliances' consumption of electricity

Consumption Per Month for Electricity		
		Kilowatts*
HEATING, AIR CONDITIONING	Home heating	1,930†
	Oil burner	50
	Furnace fan	100
	Room air conditioner	300
	Dehumidifier	67
	Humidifier	60
LIGHTING	five-room house (winter)	50
	six-room house (winter)	60
	eight-room house (winter)	80
COOKING, REFRIGERATING	Freezer (14 cu. ft.)	140
	Oven (microwave)	25
	Oven (self-cleaning)	96
	Range	100
	Refrigerator	83
	Refrigerator-freezer (frost-free)	167
LAUNDRY, HOT WATER	Dryer	80
	Iron	30
	Washer	9
	Water heater (quick recovery)	183

continued

TABLE 3.6 *continued*

Consumption Per Month for Electricity

		Kilowatts*
TV, RADIO, STEREO	Stereo	9
	Radio	8
	TV (b & w)	50
	TV (color)	100
	Computer	83
KITCHEN	Blender	1.25
	Broiler	8
	Carving knife	.66
	Coffeemaker	8
	Deep fryer	7
	Dishwasher	30
	Frying pan	15
	Hot plate	7.5
	Microwave oven	20
	Mixer	1
	Toaster	3
	Trash compactor	4
	Waffle iron	2
	Waste disposer	2.5
HEALTH BEAUTY	Shaver	.15
	Toothbrush	.04
OTHER	Battery charger	10
	Electric Blanket	22
	Clocks (4)	6
	Fan (circulating)	3.5
	Fan (window)	14
	Power tools (drill, sander)	3
	Vacuum	4
	Well pump (¾ h.p.)	20

*One kilowatt equals 1,000 watts. A 100-watt electrical item consumes 1 kilowatt in 10 hours.

†Based on 1,300 square feet: five-room house, with a year-round budget payment. Figures from Northern States Power Company and Electric Energy Association.

student check his or her estimate against the actual bill when it arrives. Afterwards, have students statistically analyze class results. It will be necessary to estimate certain aspects of this survey, such as the number of 100-watt, 75-watt, 60-watt, and 40-watt bulbs in a given house.

A preconstructed, standardized form on which data will be recorded will greatly simplify data collection and subsequent analysis. It will be important to determine precisely what kinds of data are to be collected. Children should develop the form ultimately used on the basis of class discussions.

Evaluation: successful completion of surveys

ACTIVITY FOUR:

Energy Costs

Objective: to measure and calculate energy costs

Materials: paper, pencils, and calculators

Procedure: At this point, your students should have completed a number of activities concerning the measurement of energy consumption and the cost of that consumption. They should be familiar with the kinds of data used to record and calculate such information.

It should now be possible to relate this once again to family energy consumption by having students calculate the cost of heating or electrifying their individual homes. Instruct them to find out how much money could be saved if energy conservation measures were implemented by each member of their families. You might even encourage your students to share their results with their families for possible implementation of various conservation techniques.

Evaluation: correct calculations of energy costs

ACTIVITY FIVE:

School Survey

Objective: to complete a school energy survey, and to make recommendations concerning future conservation

Materials: paper, pencils, and calculators

Procedure: Have the class conduct a schoolwide energy survey detailing fuel oil, electrical, and natural gas usage per day, week, month, and year. Small groups could be assigned to survey different sections of the school building, or to survey the various kinds of energy consumed. As with the previous surveys conducted, help students devise a form.

Following the completion of the survey, the class might be asked to develop a schoolwide plan for further energy conservation. As part of this activity, you might wish to involve the school principal, custodial engineers, and any other members of the school's personnel who might be involved in the use of energy. Have students make posters, write slogans, and create a song to remind others of the plans.

Evaluation: successful completion of the survey, and participation in group discussions and class projects to make recommendations for future conservation efforts

ACTIVITY SIX:

Energy Display

Objective: to complete a display of products of the energy conservation activities (see note following the procedure section)

Materials: varied, depending upon decisions as to the best ways to display activity results and findings

Procedure: Have the class develop an energy display that includes the results of their investigations, conclusions, and recommendations. Such a display could be made available to the general

FIGURE 3.21
Weekly home energy use sheet

	S	M	T	W	TH	F	S	Weekly Totals
# of kwh								
cost per kwh								
Total Cost								

school population, community groups, or the PTA. If this display is to be used as a major project, you may wish to expand somewhat on each of the preceding activities in terms of having the class produce lasting and attractive exhibits of their findings.

You may wish to put this display on hold until completion of the entire unit. The following activities, which for the most part will be pursued on an independent basis, will produce projects suitable for an interesting display.

Evaluation: completion and display of all related products

ACTIVITY SEVEN:

How Much Electricity Does Your Household Use at Home in One Day?

Objective: to calculate daily home electrical use

Materials: kwh meter at home (kwh: kilowatt hour)

Weekly Home Energy Sheet for each student

Procedure: Provide each student with a copy of Figure 3.21 and give them the following directions. Learn how to read a kilowatt meter, then find one in your home. Record the readings for two days. How many kilowatt hours did you use? How does your use compare with that of other families in your classroom?

Ask to see last month's electric bill. How much does 1 kwh cost?

Keep track of your family's electric use for one week. How much did each day's electricity cost?

Evaluation: ability to read electric meter and discuss the findings

ACTIVITY EIGHT:

How Much Energy Do Appliances Use?

Objective: to determine how much energy is used by various electrical appliances

Materials: kwh meter at home

several small electrical appliances

Home Appliance Electrical Usage Sheet (Figure 3.22) for each student

FIGURE 3.22

Home appliance electrical usage sheet

Appliance	# Watts Used in 2 Minutes	# kw Used in 1 Hour	Estimate # kw Used Per Month	Cost Per kwh	Estimated Cost Per Month
Microwave Oven					
Iron					
Clothes Dryer					
Computer TV					

Procedure: Provide each student with a copy of Figure 3.22 and give them the following directions.

You will need to complete this activity at home with a partner. Be sure to have permission before starting any of these activities!

1. Decide on five appliances whose electrical energy consumption you will measure.

2. Observe the kilowatt meter without any of these appliances in operation. Note particularly the change in the reading of the small wheel, which revolves continuously, after 2 minutes. This change indicates the number of watts used in the 2-minute period of time. Keep a record of this amount.

3. Now, suppose you picked a microwave oven, an iron, a clothes dryer, a computer, and a TV as your five appliances. Ask your friend at a given signal to turn on the microwave for 2 minutes. Notice the change in the meter's reading during this time. The *difference* between this amount and the one you recorded in step 2 is the amount of energy consumed by the microwave oven.

4. Repeat this process for the remaining four appliances. Record all of your results in column one of the Home Appliance Electrical Usage Sheet. Complete the other four columns before you discuss your results with other students. Were your results similar? What was the difference between the largest and the smallest estimates? What was the average estimate? Develop a plan to reduce the number of kilowatts by 10 percent.

Evaluation: completion of Home Appliance Electrical Usage Sheet

ACTIVITY NINE:

Heat Loss and House Drafts

Objective: to measure house drafts and to calculate the resulting heat losses

Materials: pencil

tape

plastic food wrap

Procedure: Provide students with the following directions.

Make a draftometer by following these directions: Cut a 10 cm by 20 cm strip of plastic food wrap. Tape it to the pencil. Your draftometer should respond to the slightest movement of air. Try it. Note: Forced air furnaces must not be in operation when you are using your draftometer!

Windows account for about 25% of heat loss. Test your windows, doors, and electrical outlets for air leakage by holding the draftometer near them, especially by the cracks. Do the same for your fireplace, if you have one. What makes the plastic wrap move? List the three places where it moves the most. Perhaps you could help to close these holes.

Evaluation: completion and use of a draftometer

ACTIVITY TEN:

How Much Energy Can Be Saved by Boiling Water in a Covered Pan?

Objective: to measure the energy saved by covering pans while cooking with them

Materials: hot plate

pan with lid

watch

water

styrofoam cups

Procedure: Provide students with the following directions.

Pour 2 cups of water into the pan. Place the pan on the hot plate and turn the hot plate on. Be careful not to touch the hot plate or pan while they are hot! Begin timing when the pan is placed on the hot plate. Record the number of minutes required for the water to boil vigorously.

Now, empty the pan and rinse it under cold water until it is thoroughly cooled. Add 2 more cups of water and cover the pan. Begin timing again when you place the pan on the hot plate. How long does it take for it to boil this time?

Now, answer these questions:

1. How did you know when the water was boiling?

2. Did covering the pan save energy?

3. Assuming that the hot plate used 1,000 watts per hour (1 kilowatt), how much money would be saved if a household heated all its water for cooking in a covered pan? (See Table 3.4.)

Evaluation: completion of experiment

ACTIVITY ELEVEN:

The Containment of Heat

Objective: to measure the containment of heat under varying conditions

Note: Activities Eleven through Seventeen can be done in pairs or groups of three. Materials are listed in quantities needed for one group.

FIGURE 3.23
Heat containment chart

TEMPERATURE READINGS					
	1 min.	2 min.	3 min.	4 min.	5 min.
Both flaps closed					
Top open, bottom closed					
Bottom open, top closed					
Both flaps open					

Materials: tall cardboard box   watch
40-watt bulb in ceramic socket   knife
thermometer   Heat Containment Chart (Figure 3.23)

Procedure: Have students follow these steps:

1. Place the bulb inside the box.
2. Cut a small hole in the bottom of the box for the cord of the lamp.
3. Make a small hole in the top of the box for the thermometer—do not put it directly over the lamp!
4. Fill in the temperature readings with flaps open and closed on the Heat Containment Chart.

Evaluation: completion of experiment

ACTIVITY TWELVE:

Paint and Temperature Loss

Objective: to determine the effect of paint on temperature loss

Materials: four juice cans
poster paint (white, black, green, red)
hot water
four thermometers
variety of food coloring
Paint and Temperature Loss Grid (Figure 3.24)

Procedure: Provide students with the following directions.
Paint each can a different color, then fill each with the same amount of very hot water. Add food coloring to the hot water.
Put a thermometer in each can. Record the temperature every 3 minutes until the water cools. Graph your results on the Paint and Temperature Loss Grid. The graphs will be more

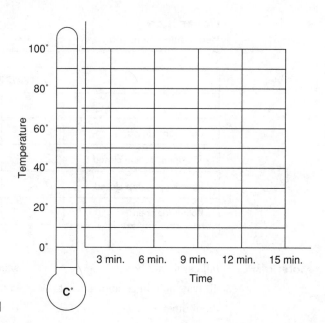

FIGURE 3.24
Paint and temperature loss grid

dramatic if the points associated with each color are connected with a pencil. You will then have four separate graphs on the same grid. The graphs can now easily be contrasted and discussed.

After you complete your graphs, answer these questions:

1. Which paint held temperature best?
2. Which are the best house paints to keep warm in winter?
3. Why aren't all houses painted this way?

Evaluation: completion of experiment

ACTIVITY THIRTEEN:

Temperature Differences in Sun and Shade

Objective: to measure the differences of water temperature in sun and shade

Materials: two styrofoam cups

two thermometers

watch or clock

Starting-Temperature Variations Chart (Figure 3.25)

Procedure: Provide students with the following directions.

Pour the same amount of very cold water into two styrofoam cups. After placing a thermometer in each cup, place one in the sun and the other in the shade. Measure the temperature and record after 5, 10, and 15 minutes.

You might want to expand this activity by using the following ideas.

FIGURE 3.25
Starting-temperature variations chart

ELAPSED TIME			
*	5 min.	10 min.	15 min.

*Use this column to give location and starting temperature.

1. Try this experiment with different-colored cups. Have students determine which color absorbs the most heat.
2. Attempt this experiment with different starting temperatures, such as 35°, 50°, and 65°F. Ask students whether the differences between beginning and ending temperatures are the same for each starting temperature. Have them enlarge and use the Starting-Temperature Variations Chart to record their results.

Evaluation: completion of experiment(s) assigned

ACTIVITY FOURTEEN:

Magnifying Glasses and Sun Spots

Objective: to determine the complications of using reflectors and lenses to collect solar energy

Materials: magnifying glass   masking tape
                      chair or stool   watch with second hand

Procedure: Select a cardboard box about 8 × 8 × 8 inches and remove the four box flaps. Cut a hole just the size of the magnifying glass in the center of one side of the box and fasten the magnifying glass over the hole securely with masking tape. Set the box on end in the sunlight and fasten a piece of white paper in the other side of the box so the sunlight passing through the lens falls on the paper. (If the disc of sunlight is larger than the magnifying glass, shorten the box until the disc of light on the paper is about one half the size of the magnifying glass.) Using a pencil, draw a line around the disc of light and write the time next to this pencil circle. Watch for several minutes.

1. Why does the disc of light move on the paper?
2. How might this relate to problems in designing solar collectors?
3. Repeat the observation at another time of day, Do you think the disc of light will take the same, more, or less time to move out of the pencil circle? Give it a try and see what happens. Can you explain why on this second try the disc took the time it took to move out of the pencil circle? Was the time the same or different on the second try?

Evaluation: completion of experiment(s) assigned

ACTIVITY FIFTEEN:

Solar Storage

Objective: to measure and compare the ability of a variety of materials to collect solar energy

Materials: cardboard box   four thermometers

black paint   sand, salt, water, and torn-up paper

four small metal cans of equal size   Solar Storage Grid (Figure 3.26)

Procedure: Provide each student with a copy of the Solar Storage Grid and give them the following directions.

Fill each can with a different material and place a thermometer in each. Get a cardboard box and paint the outside black. Put the cans in the box and place it in the sun for half an hour. Now remove the cans and watch the temperatures fall.

Take a reading every 3 minutes. Which materials' temperature falls most slowly? Graph your results on the Solar Storage Grid. Be sure to use a different-colored pencil for each material.

Evaluation: completion of experiment

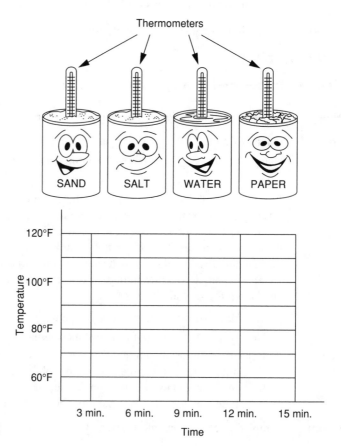

FIGURE 3.26
Solar storage grid

ACTIVITY SIXTEEN:

Measuring Friction

Objective: to measure changing friction

Materials: lunch-room trays, shoe boxes, or other containers

pencils

book or other weights

rubber bands (medium weight)

Mechanical Friction Grid (Figure 3.27)

Procedure: Provide each student with a copy of the Mechanical Friction Grid and give them the following directions.

Attach the rubber band to the lunch tray so that it can be pulled along a table-top for 2 feet. Measure how long the rubber band will stretch with the tray empty.

Now place several pounds of books or other weights on the tray and repeat the experiment. Repeat once more, doubling the amount of weight added to the tray. How far does the rubber band stretch this time?

Put three or more equally spaced round pencils or dowels under the tray. Now try pulling it. How far does the rubber band stretch this time? Graph your results on the Mechanical Friction Grid. Then try to answer these questions:

1. What does the stretched rubber band tell you about the amount of friction between the tray and the table?

2. Could you do the same experiment with a toy wagon? What do you think would happen? Try it.

3. Why do heavy cars use more gasoline than light cars?

Evaluation: completion of experiment

FIGURE 3.27
Mechanical friction grid

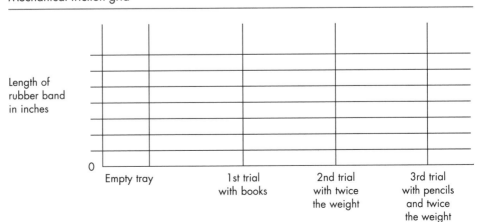

ACTIVITY SEVENTEEN:

Can You Make a Bulb Light?

Objective: to complete an electrical circuit between one or two batteries and a light bulb

Materials: two size "D" flashlight batteries

wires

small bulb

flashlight

Procedure: Have each student complete this activity using the following procedure.

1. Experiment with two wires, a battery, and a bulb. See if you can make the bulb light. Note the brightness of the light when it does appear.

Be sure to tape all wires
for the best connections.

2. Try connecting two cells to the bulb. You will need two more wires. What do you notice about the amount of light now?

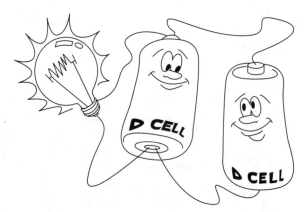

3. Can you connect a bulb and two batteries as the brightness of the bulb increases?

4. Take a flashlight apart and see if you can figure out how it works. How is it the same as your homemade flashlight made only of batteries, a bulb, and wires?

Evaluation: completion of experiment

UNIT EVALUATION: FILMSTRIP BOX

Have students use the instructions provided in Figure 3.28 to make a filmstrip box and a filmstrip that explains what they have learned about energy. Students can work in pairs, with each pair responsible for making one frame of a class filmstrip. Each frame should explain what the pair felt was the most important concept they learned about energy. Or, the class could write a story about energy by brainstorming a list of key ideas, sequencing them, and signing up in pairs to complete one frame each.

Give each pair an $8\frac{1}{2}$" × 11" sheet of paper to be used lengthwise. Each student pair should plan, edit, and recopy their sentences and visuals before they are attached together. Students can either record the script on tape or read it. A filmstrip box can be used for any unit evaluation.

ADDITIONAL ACTIVITIES:

Extension and Evaluation

1. Extend this unit by examining materials such as Free Energy Training Materials: K-3; 4-6; and 7-8. These packets each provide a wealth of energy-related materials. You can obtain them by writing to the American Gas Association, c/o Modern Talking Pictures, Inc., Dept. WLC, 5000 Park Street N., St. Petersburg, FL 33709.

2. Have students make a bulletin board or display of various types of energy.

3. Have students create hidden energy-word puzzles using a computer. Students could work on these in pairs, and the puzzles could be assembled into a class puzzle book.

4. Have students create an A–Z Book on energy conservation. Assign each student one letter to prepare.

5. Check the Internet for additional energy information and resources.

Teacher Resources

See Appendix B for resources and addresses.

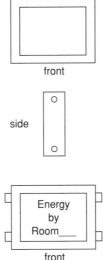

1. Cut a 9-by-11-inch hole in the bottom of a cardboard box for the screen.

front

2. Make two circles 9 inches apart on both sides of the box.
3. Make holes in the circles for the dowels to go through.

side

4. Have students tape the end of the filmstrip to the bottom dowel.
5. Roll the filmstrip onto the dowel and tape the beginning of the filmstrip to the top dowel.

FIGURE 3.28
Filmstrip box

Energy
by
Room___

front

INVENTIONS

Inventions: The activities in this unit vary widely in content and level. There is something here for everyone!

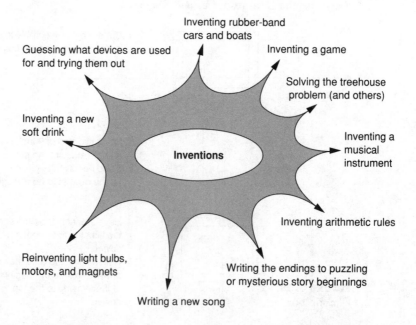

INTRODUCTION

Children at play discover many things. They find that wagons will coast downhill but must be pushed uphill. They find that a yo-yo will come back if it is spinning but will not return if it is motionless. They find that water poured onto sand at the beach soaks in rapidly, but water poured on the sidewalk forms puddles or runs off.

This unit suggests several ways of helping children learn to pose and solve problems through invention. More specifically, the unit explores some of the hows and whys of fabrications, fiction, devices, and substances, and then presents a variety of problem situations in which children are challenged to complete a story, devise an explanation, or create something that is needed.

As teachers, we know that it is difficult to structure for children learning situations in which creativity and inventiveness occur. Since it is difficult to create or invent on order, we are tempted to build learning situations in which each child succeeds at a simple task.

Therefore, on the pages that follow, you will find first three general activities to begin to get your class involved in this unit. These are followed by eight invention and discovery subtopics, each with activities that small groups can explore. Undoubtedly, your students' investigations will turn up other equally workable areas of exploration. This should be encouraged. Please remember that all of the units in this book are intended as starting points, not completed plans. All unit planning should be based largely on the characteristics and interests of your students, time, and resources available, as well as on your own areas of expertise.

Unit Objectives. Students will:

1. find out about some of the inventions and creations we enjoy and use.
2. discover that objects can have many functions.
3. understand what "to invent" means in a broad context.
4. have the freedom to create ideas, stories, poems, new objects, and new things from existing objects.

Appropriate Grade Levels. Elementary and Middle School

Vocabulary.

invention

discovery

investigation

Note: See Appendix A for planning sheets.

ACTIVITY ONE:

Pretest and Unit Introduction

Objective:	to measure general inventiveness before beginning the unit, and to introduce the unit theme. (Note: this is essentially a teacher's objective.)
Materials:	paper
	pencils, and crayons if desired

Procedure: To begin the inventions unit, give your students the following directions.

> *Pretend that your neighbors cleaned out their garage and piled up things for the garbage man to haul away. In the pile were a pair of old roller skates, a tire, some boards, several cardboard boxes, a plastic bucket, a box of mixed nails, screws and tacks, a broken tricycle, a leaky hose, and a coil of rope. You can have any of the things in the pile. Write a paragraph describing an item you could make using several of the throw-aways. Then draw a picture of it.*

Next, select one or two simple inventions (e.g., a board for carding wool, a spinning wheel, a butter churn, or a rolling pin) and present them to your class while explaining that these items were used when the related tasks still had to be done by hand. Mention some tasks that are still done by hand (e.g., folding letters to go into envelopes, tying shoelaces, and peeling oranges) and ask students whether there is an invention or device that might do each of these tasks.

At the same time, be sure to explain to children that inventions aren't just limited to devices that perform particular tasks. Inventions in a broad context include verbal fabrications, fiction, new art forms, new solutions to problems, and new songs as well as new devices and substances. To conclude this unit introduction, you may wish to present stories without endings for students to complete or puzzles for students to solve as a means to stimulate inventiveness.

Evaluation: completion of assignments, participation in group activities and discussions

ACTIVITY TWO:

Beginning Research

Objective: to find and use resource materials related to inventing

Materials: a variety of resource materials in your school library

Producer: As further preparation for the unit, send your class to the library or school resource center. Ask the librarian or media specialist to set up a cart of books, games, puzzles, etc. that relate to inventions and could be kept in your classroom for a few days. You might instead want to simply give your students directions that will help them locate appropriate resource materials for themselves.

Upon returning to your classroom, put the webbing diagram from the opening page of this unit on the board or have your students create a web of their own. From this, allow students time during which they can explore their resources and begin to identify possible projects.

Evaluation: successful location and perusal of library materials related to inventions

ACTIVITY THREE:

Project Planning

Objective: to begin planning group projects and to collect related materials

Materials: variable, depending upon projects identified

Procedure: At this point, all of your students should have had time to seek out and look through a variety of resource materials. They now need to divide into small groups, each of which can identify an invention or category of inventions on which they wish to work as a group. Perhaps the best way to divide the class is to have students contribute project ideas to a class list, and then organize children according to their project choice. Another method would be to set up groups first and then allow time for each group to choose one project to be completed.

Once groups have identified the invention on which they wish to work, your task will be to help children with suggestions, ideas, sources of information, and materials needed for construction. However, be sure to encourage groups to plan their investigations before you make suggestions. When students seek help from you, suggestions in the form of questions can help direct their thoughts and encourage alternative approaches so that the students are ultimately finding their own answers and solutions.

Once each group of students has selected a project idea or area, suggest that they consider several related investigations. For example, if the children in one group choose "Inventing a Soft Drink," one of the general topics listed for exploration in subsequent pages of this unit, they could find out about two or more of the following:

1. soft drink flavors

2. carbonation and CO_2

3. history of the development of the soft drink industry

4. natural and artificial flavors

5. bottles, cans, and recycling

6. trademarks

7. inventing a new flavor

Help each group to first choose a few themes of high interest for study and then develop daily plans for the following 2 or 3 days. Discuss with them the nature of the final report on the invention or discovery that you will expect from each group. You will find it helpful to have each group submit a set of plans and a description of their proposed report in advance. Such plans will not only help you keep track of progress, but will also be useful guides for the students themselves. In addition, these written plans should be useful evaluation guides for both you and your students.

You may also want to make some related assignments, such as the development of reports or minibooks in which students describe their experiences or discuss other inventions that fit into the same category as the topic they have chosen. For example, a group making rubber-band cars could make a collage of auto pictures and describe a variety of cars and their histories.

Finally, if possible, the children's completed inventions should be displayed in a central location of the school so their ideas and creations can be shared with other students.

Evaluation: project plan submitted by each group

ACTIVITY FOUR AND BEYOND:

Eight Invention and Discovery Areas

The following pages contain activity suggestions for a variety of general topics related to invention and discovery. As explained in the unit introduction, this is certainly not a complete or all-inclusive list of possible fields of exploration. Rather, it is intended to be used by you as a set of examples that show how students can branch out within a general topic of interest and study.

The general planning and implementation procedures for these eight activities have been outlined within Activity Three. The topics for investigation included here are

1. automobiles
2. games
3. music
4. numbers
5. stories
6. songs
7. soft drinks
8. inventions that are needed

For each topic, the objective of the activities will be the completion of the identified projects, and materials will be dependent upon the project undertaken. Evaluation is then based on completion of the project and perhaps on the planning that precedes it.

ACTIVITY FOUR:

Automobiles

1. Set up a toy auto display showing the make and year of several cars.
2. Make posters or drawings of automobiles, dream cars, racing cars, modified cars, dune buggies, and others.
3. Find out what makes automobiles go, including information on gasoline-, diesel-, and battery-powered cars.
4. Research what percent of a newspaper is devoted to autos by measuring the space taken up by articles, feature advertisements, classified advertisements, and parts ads.
5. Write and/or read stories about autos.
6. Write and/or sing songs about autos.
7. Do research on foreign automobiles, their makes, and history.
8. Find out about automobile racing and stunt driving.
9. Build scale model autos from kits.
10. Construct rubber-band-driven autos or create vehicles using Tinkertoys. Solve problems related to connecting rubber bands, wheel friction, axle construction, and so on.
11. Hold auto races and measure the speed of the cars used. One way to do this is to lay out a marked track on the floor. Use a clock, watch, or one-second pendulum to measure the speed of the cars.

$$speed = \frac{distance\ travelled}{time}$$

Example:

$$speed = \frac{6\ meters}{4\ seconds} = 1.5\ meters\ per\ second$$

ACTIVITY FIVE:

Games

1. Find as many kinds of puzzles and games as possible. Find out what the difference is between a game and a puzzle.

2. Research the types and rules of a wide variety of games, including card games, board games, and playground games.

3. Find out about a variety of puzzles, including interlocking and number combinations such as Magic Squares and others.

4. Create and play games and puzzles intended for one or two players or for teams.

5. Compare games of strategy (checkers, Chinese checkers, and chess) and games of chance (those that use spinners, card turning, or dice).

6. Learn about the psychology of games. For example, try to answer the questions, "Can you play a game better if you practice? Can you flip a coin or roll a dice better with practice?" Plan a study to find out whether practice can improve one's ability in either chance or skill games.

7. Study the mathematics of chance. Dice in particular offer some interesting investigations. Some examples follow:
   a. Roll a single die (six sides numbered 1 through 6). Keep a record of the number of times each face comes up in 10, 50, and 75 rolls. Predict the number of times each face will come up in 100 rolls.
   b. Roll two dice. Keep a record of the number of times 2s, 3s, 4s, and so on through 12s are rolled. Make a histogram of 100 rolls.
   c. Devise a chance table for two dice showing how many times each sum (2 through 12) can be expected to appear in 72 rolls.

8. Invent a game. First, complete a description table indicating the game's object; whether it is based on chance or skill; number of players; whether cards, a board, or other pieces are necessary; what other game it is like; how many minutes it takes to play; and what you will learn by playing the game.

9. Invent a puzzle involving a maze or pieces. Find out what skills are needed, such as fitting parts together, and what kind of other puzzle it is like.

ACTIVITY SIX:

Making a Musical Instrument

1. Make a list of all the musical instruments you know. Divide the instruments according to how they make sounds. Describe different ways sounds are made (i.e., oboe—wind, strings—friction, drums—pounding).

2. Find out how sirens work. Make one using a piece of cardboard, a hole-punch, and a straw. Use a Tinkertoy support. Find out what makes the siren loud or soft, and high or low in pitch.

3. Make three lists of instruments. First, list instruments that make mostly low sounds. Second, list those that make mostly high-pitched sounds. Third, list instruments that produce both low and high sounds.

4. Make a bottle xylophone. Tune bottles by partly filling them with water, each to a different level. Try creating a variety of tones by tapping the bottles with a wooden mallet and a metal spoon, or by blowing over the tops of the bottles.

5. Make a one-string guitar, using a board, two eye-screws, and a piece of fine wire stretched between the screws. The wire can be tightened by twisting one of the eye-screws. Cut strips of wood for frets and set them in place so you can shorten the string and play different notes.

6. Make a tub bass, using a large metal can, an old bucket, or an old washtub. You also will need a strong piece of cord, two pieces of wood, and a nail. Fasten the cord to the center of the tub using a short stick. The cord can be tightened by pressing down on the stick.

7. Make a bazooka from a piece of 1-inch plastic pipe and two round pieces of wood.

8. Invent a new instrument that will play several notes.

ACTIVITY SEVEN:

Inventing Number Patterns and Arithmetic Rules

1. Design Magic Squares. For example, in the following square, the numbers in each row and the numbers in each column add up to 12. But the diagonal numbers add up to 7 and 17. Can you substitute numbers so the diagonals, too, will add up to 12? Can you now use the numbers 1, 2, 3, 4, 5, 6, 7, 8, and 9 in each of the cells so that the rows, columns, and diagonals will all add up to 15? Is it possible to arrange the numbers so that the four corners, too, add up to 15? Try the numbers 10, 11, 12, 13, 14, 15, 16, 17, and 18. How about 11 through 19? Invent a new Magic Square with a five-by-five matrix. When you are an expert, try a four-by-four Magic Square using the numbers 1 through 16. Warning: This can be very difficult!

2	4	6
3	4	5
7	4	1

2. Make discoveries using a hand-held calculator. Construct a matrix like the one following to change fractions to decimals, and write the answers in the matrix. Can you see any patterns? Before the matrix is complete, can you predict some of the decimals? Try several other matrices using different numerators and denominators.

		DENOMINATOR		
		6	7	8	9
	6	$\frac{6}{6} = 1$	$\frac{6}{7} = .8571$	$\frac{6}{8} = .75$	$\frac{6}{9} = .6666$
	5	$\frac{5}{6} = .8333$	$\frac{5}{7} = .7412$	$\frac{5}{8} = .625$	$\frac{5}{9} =$
NUMERATOR	4	$\frac{4}{6} = .6666$	$\frac{4}{7} = .5714$	$\frac{4}{8} = .5$	$\frac{4}{9} =$
	3	$\frac{3}{6} = .5$	$\frac{3}{7} = .4286$	$\frac{3}{8} =$	$\frac{3}{9} =$
	2	$\frac{2}{6} = .3333$	$\frac{2}{7} = .2857$	$\frac{2}{8} =$	$\frac{2}{9} =$
	1	$\frac{1}{6} = .16666$	$\frac{1}{7} =$	$\frac{1}{8} =$	$\frac{1}{9} =$

3. Make some more hand-held calculator discoveries. Once you think you see a pattern, guess the answer before you press the = button.

$1 \times 11 = $ _____ $10 \times 11 = $ _____

$2 \times 11 = $ _____ $11 \times 11 = $ _____

$3 \times 11 = $ _____ $100 \times 11 = $ _____

$4 \times 11 = $ _____ $101 \times 11 = $ _____

$5 \times 11 = $ _____

Without using your calculator, predict the decimal equivalents of the following:

	Guess	*Press*
5/11	_____	_____
6/11	_____	_____
7/11	_____	_____
8/11	_____	_____
9/11	_____	_____
10/11	_____	_____

4. Complete calculator sevenths. Use your calculator to find the decimal equivalents to six places for these fractions:

$1/7 = $ _____ $4/7 = $ _____

$2/7 = $ _____ $5/7 = $ _____

$3/7 = $ _____ $6/7 = $ _____

Can you find a sequence of digits and a pattern that would help you write the decimal for any seventh?
Can you find a rule that will help you predict the equivalents for these:

$8/7 = $ _____ $15/7 = $ _____

$9/7 = $ _____ $16/7 = $ _____

$10/7 = $ _____ $17/7 = $ _____

$11/7 = $ _____ $18/7 = $ _____

5. Complete more calculator fraction patterns. Work the following problems with your calculator. Write the first six digits of each answer in the corresponding column in the table. Look at the first and fourth columns. What patterns do you see? Compare the second and fifth columns. What do you notice? Compare the third and sixth columns. Can you guess what numbers would be in the seventh column? Check your guesses using your calculator. What is the sum of the numbers in the first row? The last row? What about the other rows? Expand the table to include $7 \div 13$, $8 \div 13$, and so on. Are the patterns the same? Can you predict the decimal equivalent for $12 \div 13$, and so on?

	FIRST	SECOND	THIRD	FOURTH	FIFTH	SIXTH
1 ÷ 13						
2 ÷ 13						
3 ÷ 13						
4 ÷ 13						
5 ÷ 13						
6 ÷ 13						

6. Collect at least six discs. Jar lids, plates, can tops, and wheels can be used. Measure the distance across each and the distance around each in cm. Chart your data in the following table:

Disc	1	2	3	4	5	6
Distance around						
Distance across						
Distance around ÷ distance across						

7. Count out 100 toothpicks. Draw parallel lines on a large sheet of paper. The lines should be exactly one toothpick-length apart. Hold the toothpicks about 1 meter above the center of the paper and drop them one at a time. Keep a record of the number of toothpicks that touch one of the parallel lines. How many touched a line? How many did you drop? What number do you get when you divide the number that touched a line into the number dropped? Try again and see if you get about the same number. Can you tell why you get this number each time?

ACTIVITY EIGHT:

Writing Endings to Stories

1. Collect comic strips from several newspapers. Cut and paste white paper over the word boxes. Then, reorder the pictures and write new dialogue. They can be used for announcements, bulletin boards, or funny or sad stories.

2. Collect magazine pictures and mount them on one side of a page. Arrange them so they tell a story. Across from each picture, write one or two paragraphs of the story.

3. Cut full-page advertisements from magazines. Cut and paste white paper over the captions and writing. Write new captions and descriptions. Some can be funny, some mysterious, some ridiculous.

4. Get an old reader that no one uses anymore. Carefully cut out the pages and separate a short story. Rewrite parts of the story or the end of the story. Cut out paragraphs that are

not needed and replace them with the ones you've written. Staple the new story together with a construction-paper cover.

5. Make add-on stories. Have each person in your group write the first paragraph of a story. Then exchange papers and each person will write a second paragraph. Continue until each story is complete. Hang up the stories so everyone can read them.

6. Have your teacher select an interesting story and read about half of it to you. Then, in a group, plan the remainder of the story and have each one in your group select a paragraph of the second half to write. When you are finished, the story can be read aloud or placed conveniently so everyone can read it.

7. Select one of the short super-8-mm film cartridges provided by your teacher and watch it on a projector. Then write a narrative and devise sound effects for appropriate parts of the film. Use a tape recorder to make the sound track for the film. Share your final production with the entire class.

ACTIVITY NINE:

Songs

1. Work with a partner. Write out the words to a simple song you both know, one line at a time. Then sing the song and underline each word or part of a word that corresponds with a beat of the music. Now, using the same beat pattern, write a new verse to the melody.

2. This time, start with a verse you don't know. Underline the beats in the verse and try several melodies until you discover one that matches the beat. If you can, record it on a cassette and teach it during music class.

3. Write your own music and match it with a poem. Or, write both the words and music for a new song. Teach it to a friend.

ACTIVITY TEN:

Inventing a New Soft Drink

1. How often have you wished for a new soft drink flavor? Create a new flavor by mixing two or more soft drinks together, keeping careful records of proportions used. You can use orange, strawberry, grape, lemon-lime, cola, or any other flavor you like. You will need several paper cups and a measuring cup. Once you have invented several new drink flavors, have other students taste each and record preferences. You might also like to create names for your new beverages and draw posters to advertise them.

2. What makes the fizz in soft drinks? Learn about carbonation and CO_2.

3. Find out about and compare artificial and natural flavors and sweeteners.

4. Conduct a survey of soft drink flavor preferences, comparing choices according to age and gender.

5. Study the history and development of the soft drink industry. Find out how long people have been drinking soft drinks, where they were first manufactured, and so on.

6. Find out about soft drink packaging and recycling of bottles and cans. Plan and carry out a recycling program in your class, school, home, or neighborhood.

ACTIVITY ELEVEN:

Surveying for Needed Inventions

Categorize the things you do during the day, and record these on a sheet of paper. Ask other children and adults to think of an item or device they use in any of the categories that needs to be improved or a not-yet-invented item or device that would be useful to them. You may wish to include the following category headings:

Clothing	Beverages
Toys and Sports Equipment	Cooking Equipment
Transportation	Home Items
Food	Containers

Now, reduce the list to include only the items that were mentioned several times. Select one suggested or needed item and design such an item. Your design should include a drawing and a description.

UNIT EVALUATION: A–Z BIG BOOK

Have students make a class A–Z big book about inventions. Write each letter of the alphabet on a slip of paper, put the slips in a bag, and have each student draw one. Students will then each make a page for the book based on the letter they drew. Each page must include at least five words and two visuals related to inventions, as illustrated in Figure 3.29. An A–Z big book can be used for any unit evaluation.

ADDITIONAL ACTIVITIES:

Extension and Evaluation

1. Have your students explore the lives of famous inventors. They can then create written or oral reports or pictorial displays from their findings. If they choose, allow students to complete this activity based on their fellow classroom inventors.

Our A-Z
BIG BOOK
OF
INVENTIONS
by Room____

airplane
Wright brothers
Leonardo da Vinci
wings
windshear

FIGURE 3.29
A to Z big book

2. Ask students to create a list of the most important inventions ever created. Have each student choose one of these inventions and explore its effect on human society. Direct them to predict how civilization might have developed differently had that item not been invented.

3. An exploration of science fiction literature can turn up a wide array of imagined inventions. Your students might search older science fiction books to find devices that have now been built, or they might predict which of those from current literature may become actual objects in the future. Finally, encourage them to create possible future inventions in drawings, writings, or three-dimensional representations.

4. Have pairs of students use the computer to create a hidden-word puzzle based on inventions or inventors. Duplicate the puzzles and place them in a learning center for others to solve.

5. Have students make a time line of important inventions. Students could work in teams, with each team responsible for a century.

6. Have students choose inventors and prepare 5-minute speeches about their lives and inventions. Students could come dressed as their inventors. Or, they could work in pairs and present the information in an interview format. You might want to tape these interviews with a videocamera.

7. Make a classroom display of books about inventors and inventions.

Teacher Resources

Inventions by R. Smith. Cypress, CA: Creative Teaching Press, 1992. (literature-based activities for thematic teaching)

Inventions by Karen Goldfluss and Patricia Sim. Huntington Beach, CA: Teacher Created Materials, Inc., 1993. (thematic unit)

The Inventor Series, Greenhaven Press.

The African-American Inventors Series, Milbrook Press.

The Timeline Inventions Series, Franklin Watts.

See Appendix B for additional resources and addresses.

MNEMONICS

Mnemonics: This theme contains a wide variety of activities designed to assist in the memorization of school-related lists, names, arithmetic facts, capitals, spelling words, and rules. Special consideration is given to mnemonic devices for learning multiplication facts.

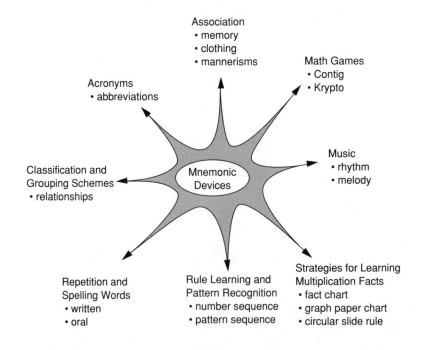

INTRODUCTION

It is useful to think about memory as relating to two different kinds of learning outcomes: knowledge stating and rule application. The former implies the preservation and retention of knowledge and meaning, as well as the ability to accurately relay such information to others. The latter, as its name implies, deals with the ability to use knowledge in an applied setting. This may require the individual to synthesize previously learned information and apply it to new problem situations. Both kinds of outcomes have an important place in the educational setting.

The activities included in this unit are designed to provide children with procedures that should simplify the task of memorizing specific information. Some of the items to be memorized will lack conceptual connections with previously learned information. This undoubtedly is the most difficult kind of material to memorize. Examples of these free-floating bits of information are names of people, places, and things; specific descriptive information about these; definitions; words of songs and poems; and *some* aspects of the interrelationships among elements in the real world (i.e., the fact that the bee is responsible for pollinating a wide variety of fruits and flowers).

The ability to recall is dependent upon the strength of the original association (implanting the item in memory), and by the interval between the time of learning and the time of retrieval. The strength of the original association usually determines whether an item is placed in long-term or short-term memory. The amount of forgetting is dependent upon these same two factors. These facts have tremendous implications for instruction.

If we expect children to remember things, then we must focus on the degree of impact that the material to be recalled has upon the individual at the time it is being encoded. Meaning, understanding, and self-construction are all factors that tend to accentuate the impact of the initial encoding. Beyond these, there are mnemonic devices that can be utilized to aid students with memorization tasks. The sample lessons that follow are illustrative of how helpful these devices can be. You may enjoy developing other activities within each of the categories mentioned.

Unit Objective. Students will learn a variety of procedures to simplify the memorization of specific information. These procedures will include rule learning, pattern recognition, repetition, and classification.

Appropriate Grade Levels. Elementary and Middle School

Vocabulary.

mnemonic

acronym

acrostic

Note: See Appendix A for planning sheets.

ACTIVITY ONE:

Repetition and Spelling Words: Written or Oral?

Objective: to learn an effective method for the memorization of spelling words

Materials: paper and pencils

Procedure: How do you learn? When asked this question, children aged 7 to 10 in Burnsville, Minnesota, generated the following list:

observing	writing	TV
pictures and drawings	research	Internet
reading	copying	movies
experimenting	asking questions	computers
surveying	listening to teachers	

In addition to these, memorization of isolated facts is often accomplished through repetitive tasks of various kinds.

A fourth-grade class in Iowa City generated the following procedures specifically for learning spelling words:

1. flash words on a screen (or use flash cards)
2. write the word several times
3. read and study
4. make sentences using the words
5. write definitions
6. write a story using the words
7. have a practice test
8. have a spelling bee

This activity involves an experiment designed to test the relative effectiveness of two kinds of repetitive procedures on learning a list of spelling words. The two procedures are the use of flash cards with verbal repetition and the recopying of words in a notebook. A third procedure will combine both of these.

First, select an appropriate list of words to be learned. One such list used in the fourth-grade class in Iowa City included these words:

escape	paralyze
luxury	concern
mosquito	stubborn
neighbor	across
occurrence	discuss

Second, select student subjects who will be exposed to the three treatments. Pretest all subjects to be sure that they do not already know how to spell all the words on the spelling list used. Divide these students into three groups.

Next, make flash cards for each word, and then ask one group to view the flash cards and spell the words aloud. Repeat this procedure 10 times. In the meantime, the second group should recopy each word in their notebooks 10 times. Ask the third group to orally spell the word five times and then to recopy each word in their notebooks five times.

Your last step is to give all three treatment groups a post-test consisting of the 10 words in random order. Record the results, figuring average scores for each group. It might be interesting to share and discuss the results with the whole class. You should also administer a retention test in 3 or 4 days, again recording and discussing the results with the class.

Evaluation: completion of tests, participation in class discussions and any activities associated with the group's study method

ACTIVITY TWO:

Association: What Was His Name Again?

Objective: memorizing students' names by using associations

Materials: none needed

Procedure: Often, memory can be enhanced by forcing a mental association between the item to be remembered and some overt characteristic of that item. Such a technique is often used by persons credited with having outstanding memories. You have, no doubt, heard of the person who has been introduced to a room full of people and remembers everyone's name for the rest of the evening. The ability to remember in this way can enormously contribute to one's social poise and is obviously worth some attention. It is usually accomplished using mental associations.

Give your students a chance to practice associative memory techniques. When they are trying to remember the names of people, for example, urge them to make a conscious effort to mentally connect a person's name with some obvious characteristic of that person, such as clothing or mannerisms. For example, Barbara might be wearing a blue blouse. In addition to this kind of association, encourage children to use the individual's name in conversation whenever appropriate and initially to think of the name or some characteristic whenever they look at the person. You will be amazed at how much students' ability to remember names will improve with a little practice.

A procedure that students can use to remember other students' names on the first day of class involves continuous repetition of ever-expanding sequences of names and faces. Using this procedure, it is possible to learn 30 names in about 20 to 25 minutes. The procedure is as follows. First, have all the students make and display name tags on their blouses or shirts. Next, have each student select two or three other students, mentally associating their names and faces, and have them do this until they feel quite comfortable with the new names. Then students should expand the list by one name, repeating the above procedure. They should continue until they can associate the names and faces of all the other students. Order is not important after four or five names have been memorized.

The ability to recall people's names on Monday, however, does not guarantee that one will be able to do it again on Tuesday. Explain to your class that steps must be taken to repeat the entire procedure once or twice more. The second and third times are obviously much easier. By the third time, students will probably miss only one or two names. Finally, to firmly plant these names in long-term memory, students need use them only in normal activity as the opportunities arise.

One last point is worth noting. To conduct the above activity, it is obvious that the person doing the remembering must devote his or her full attention to the task. If that person is you, the teacher, engage children in group work or individual projects of some type while you conduct the activity. If the students are the ones involved, all class members can do it at the same time. Simply have them assemble in the center of the room in a group activity.

Evaluation: ability to name all the students in the class

ACTIVITY THREE:

A Pocket Full Of . . .

Objective: to combine repetition and association to improve memory

Materials: set of cards, marked with the items to be memorized

two pockets or containers for each game

paper and pencils

Procedure: This activity utilizes both repetition and association. The general idea can be used to help students memorize basic factual information such as names of people, places, and things, or poetry, songs, or virtually any item of interest.

First, decide what is to be learned. As an example, you might use a word-picture association between the names of plants and their pictures. On one side of the card, you would print the name of the plant, and on the other paste its picture. Do this for all plants, or other items, on your list.

Then place the completed cards in one pocket. The object is for each student to transfer all the cards to the second pocket and back again. A single card can be transferred only if the correct name of the plant is supplied. If it is not named correctly, the card is replaced in the same pocket at the back of the stack. When all cards have been moved to the second pocket, students repeat the procedure. By the time all cards are back where they started, it is likely that the information has been memorized, since each item has been successfully identified on two different occasions. Note that this activity requires only a small period of spare time. As little as 2 or 3 minutes can be utilized to run through a small number of cards.

This game is solitary in nature and places one in competition only with oneself. The gimmick of moving cards from one pocket to another will motivate many children to learn the information.

If a large number of cards is involved, you may want to categorize the information first, asking students to work with one section at a time. In addition, if long-term memorization is the objective, this entire procedure will need to be repeated sporadically. The frequency of such repetition will be dependent upon the capabilities of the child involved.

Some types of items that can be learned using this procedure include the following:

1. names of animals and birds

2. facts about plants and animals

3. states and their capitals

4. number facts (e.g., addition and subtraction)

5. poetry and songs

6. specific facts about virtually anything

Evaluation: placement of all cards into the beginning pocket or container, indicating memorization of all items presented

ACTIVITY FOUR:

Rule Learning and Pattern Recognition

Objective: to use rules and patterns to improve memorization

Materials: paper and pencils, if desired

Procedure   Remembering rules and patterns is much more efficient than learning isolated numbers. This is because in many cases (though not all), the isolated numbers can be thought of as being specific examples of a particular rule or pattern. For example, consider the following number sequence: 71421283542. It would be difficult to remember this sequence if the task were approached without attempting to find some structure or pattern. Further, it would be impossible to predict the next number in the sequence (which, incidentally, is 4) unless some type of meaning was attached to it.

As soon as one realizes that any number in the sequence can be generated simply by adding 7 to the previous number (i.e., 7 14 21 28), the pattern becomes clear and can be continued indefinitely. In this case, however, we are not remembering the sequence but rather the rule that generates that sequence.

The economy of this type of endeavor should be very clear. One rule or pattern permits immediate access to an infinite sequence of numbers. This is sometimes referred to as understanding, and it has tremendous implications for what we do with children. Too often, time is spent remembering isolated bits when that same time could be used more productively searching for the more general and more powerful rule or pattern.

The generation or the discovery of rules or patterns by children is an incredibly important intellectual endeavor and one most worthy of expanded attention in schools. In order to build skills of this type, you should provide opportunities for children to examine lists and search for patterns. When you begin, you may find yourself providing all of the answers. After several repetitions, however, at least some of your students will begin to identify those rules or patterns themselves.

Evaluation: successful naming of sequences of numbers or items presented, and/or the ability to identify the rule or pattern in a sequence

ACTIVITIES FIVE AND SIX:*

Music and Memorization, An Introduction

Activities that use melody, rhythm, or melody plus rhythm (music) may be structured to help students recall sequentially ordered numbers, letters, objects, or events. Some general ideas for combining musical elements and items to be memorized include the following:

1. melody with telephone numbers
2. rhythm with spelling
3. rhythm with science facts (e.g., bones in the body or flower parts)
4. music with arithmetic facts (e.g., addition or subtraction)

The following two activities will look individually at the musical components of melody and rhythm as they affect memory.

---

*The authors are indebted to their colleague in Music Therapy at the University of Texas, Professor Judith Jellison, for her contributions to Activities Five and Six.

ACTIVITY FIVE:

Rhythm and Memorization

Objective: to use rhythm to aid memorization of the spelling of the names of states (or any other list)

Materials: simple rhythm instruments, if desired (tambourines, rhythm sticks)

Procedure: To illustrate this procedure, the spelling of states in the United States could be coupled with rhythm. While the use of rhythm may not be necessary or appropriate to teach the spelling of all of the states, it may be helpful for learning those that tend to be the most difficult for many students.

Have students look at a selected list of the states, including Ohio. You then will clap four slow and even beats. Ask students to select a state from the list that best fits the rhythm you have clapped. They will probably select Ohio because it has four letters. Now, both the students and you should clap while spelling Ohio in a slow and even four-beat rhythm. When the entire class claps, students should use only two fingers to clap in the palm of the other hand. This enables the spelling of the states to be heard.

The students should then select another state from the list that they would like to hear spelled in rhythm. You will clap the new state's name in rhythm, making sure to keep the rhythm in a pattern that fits the four beats or repeated four-beat patterns (8s, 12s) of Ohio. Examples are as follows:

1	2	3	4	5	6	7	8
O	K	L	A	H	O	M	A
C	O	L	O	R	A	D	O
A	R	K	A	N	S	A	S

You and your students should clap and spell the new state rhythm together. Spend time with each rhythm in variations (e.g., clapping without spelling, spelling in rhythm without clapping, half the class, and individuals) before introducing new rhythms.

Once a new rhythm is learned, combine that rhythm with the Ohio rhythm as indicated above. You may choose to use instruments after, and only after, the students do well with clapping. More difficult combinations then may be attempted. In any case, be sure to keep a strong leader in front for each state rhythm group while you maintain the strong, four-beat Ohio rhythm.

Evaluation: correct clapping of rhythms presented, correct spelling of state names presented for learning

ACTIVITY SIX:

Melody and Memorization

Objective: to use melody to aid memorization of telephone numbers, or of any lists desired

Materials: melody instrument(s)

Procedure: The use of melody to assist in recall of an emergency telephone number is a further example of mnemonics. The telephone number used should be written on the board. Have students identify the direction of the notes in the melody from the numbers, with direction indicated by the magnitude of the number. For example, 633-1827 would result melodically in the starting note 6—down 3—same 3—down 1—up 8—down 2—up 7.

You should sing or play the starting note for the first number on a melody instrument. Following the melody pattern, students then create melodies and present them to the class through singing or playing on melody instruments.

The class can determine the "best" melody and practice singing this newly created tune. To help students retain this learning, have them sing the melody periodically throughout the year.

Evaluation: correct naming, in sequence, of numbers of items presented for memorization, correct use of melody system with identified items

ACTIVITY SEVEN:

Acronyms

Objective: to use acronyms to aid memorization

Materials: none needed

Procedure: An acronym is a word formed from the initial letter or letters of each of the successive parts or major parts of a compound term. Both abbreviations and acronyms have been used as aids to memory for many years. Abbreviations, of which acronyms are a form, have been found on the earliest-known tombs, monuments, and coins. Before the printing press was invented, when manuscripts were written by hand, many abbreviations were used to save time and space. Hundreds of Latin abbreviations are still used.

Some commonly used abbreviations and acronyms include the following:

AAA	American Automobile Association
CPA	Certified Public Accountant
NATO	North Atlantic Treaty Organization
VIP	Very Important Person

Others that may have been a part of your past include the following:

HOMES	The names of the Great Lakes
ROYGBIV	The names and order of the colors of the spectrum
Every Good Boy Does Fine	The names of the lines of the musical staff

To make use of this memory technique, encourage children to construct their own acronyms and abbreviations for sequences that need to be memorized. Share these orally or by creating some type of room display. With a little encouragement, students can have a great deal of fun with this while also building their store of learned information.

Evaluation: correct recall of acronyms presented, sharing of created acronyms

ACTIVITY EIGHT:

Acrostic

Objective: to use an acrostic to aid memorization

Materials: none needed

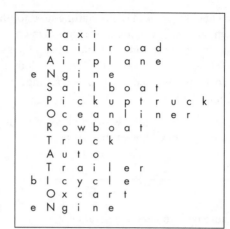

FIGURE 3.30
Transportation acrostic

Procedure: An acrostic is a way to help students organize information about a particular topic. For example, choose the word *transportation*. Write the word vertically on the chalkboard or a piece of paper. Have students brainstorm types of transportation whose names begin with or include each letter in *transportation*. The class should come up with an acrostic similar to the one in Figure 3.30.

Evaluation: successful completion of an acrostic

ACTIVITY NINE:

Fact Chart

Objective: to learn multiplication facts through the use of a 10 × 10 fact chart

Materials: copy of chart for each student from your math book

pencils and scissors

Procedure: A very useful tool for students from the time they begin to develop an awareness of multiplication until all the basic facts are memorized is the basic fact chart.

The chart is built as students progress. It should *not* be given to them already filled in to be memorized. In the early learning stages, the chart may only be large enough to accommodate factors and products through $5 \times 5 = 25$. As students develop the product relationships through various means (e.g., arrays, number lines, and cross products), results are placed on the chart. It should be expanded to full size as the need for larger products arises.

Using the chart as a reference tool provides continuous reinforcement and will encourage retention of the facts. To use the chart to its best advantage, each student should make one. Individual charts may be mounted on tagboard and kept in the students' math books or taped to the top of their desks.

As students mature and are ready to be weaned from dependence upon the chart (be sure about this readiness), try this next step on an individual basis. Set goals with the children to commit the facts to memory. They will undoubtedly know half or more already. Determine this by administering a test on the facts. Those facts that are already known can be cut away from each chart. Be sure before cutting that a border is left around the chart so that it won't fall apart when it is cut.

Set a schedule with the children for the next testing. The interval used could be weekly, biweekly, or whatever you think is appropriate. After each test, snip away the known facts. In this way, the pupils will be competing only against themselves. Individual progress will thus be very visible. The cut-up chart quickly shows that the number of facts requiring concentration is becoming lower and lower after each testing.

This process can also be extended by using a completed multiplication chart to find the corresponding division facts. The inverse relationship between multiplication and division is emphasized when the chart is used in this way.

Example:

$48 \div 6 = ?$ Find 48 in the field of products. Find the 6 either at the left or at the top. Find the missing factor in the corresponding top or left row.

Evaluation: correct naming of all multiplication facts (and division facts if applicable)

ACTIVITY TEN:

Graph-Paper Chart

Objective: to complete a graph-paper chart for multiplication facts

Materials: graph paper   crayons

Procedure: When graph-paper squares are colored in, a vivid pattern of multiplication facts appears. Have students color in the second row of squares to show the product of $1 \times 1, 1 \times 2$, and 1×3. Have them leave one square blank around each product. Next, have them color blocks to show $2 \times 1, 2 \times 2$, and 2×3. Be sure that one row is left blank between each product. The pattern will look like the one shown in Figure 3.31.

Examination of the colored blocks reveals multiplication facts as regions of various sizes. Special regions are along the major diagonal starting with the 1×1 block, these regions all being square in shape. By looking at the two halves of the chart when a diagonal line is drawn from corner to corner, students can see pairings of regions to illustrate the commutative property.

To make other discoveries, have students extend the paper and complete blocks beyond 6×6. If this activity is done on larger-scale graph-paper, it can become a good group project for class display.

Evaluation: correct completion of graph-paper chart, ability to correctly answer questions concerning the patterns it shows

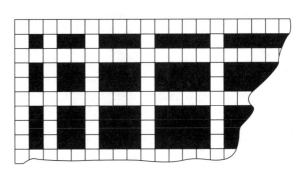

FIGURE 3.31
Multiplication-fact pattern

ACTIVITY ELEVEN:

Using a Circular Slide Rule for Multiplication and Division

Objective: to construct and correctly use a circular slide rule for multiplication and division computations

Materials: a copy of the two slide-rule components (Figure 3.32) for each child

thumbtacks

corks, tape, or small pieces of soft wood

Procedure: This particular slide rule has been modified slightly (numbers through 100 included) from the engineer's rule.

In this activity, the slide rule is used to generate products to 100, although its use can be extended further. The circular rule illustrated in Figure 3.32 should be reproduced for student use. Have each student cut out both circles, place a thumbtack (point up) precisely through the cross hairs in the center of each rule, and place a cork, piece of tape, or small piece of soft wood on top of the tack. The inner rule should rotate smoothly within the outer rule.

When this is completed, instruct students on the use of this device. For example, show them how to multiply 6 × 8 (a similar procedure is used for all problems of the form $a \times b = n$, where a and b are known). Explain orally, or provide in written form, the following steps:

1. Locate the first factor on the outside rule. (6)
2. Place the 1 of the inside rule directly under the number identified in step 1. (6)
3. Locate the second factor on the inside scale. (8)
4. Read the product on the outside scale directly opposite the second factor on the inside scale. (48)

Provide many similar problems to the class so that each student can practice and learn this technique.

This circular rule can also help to show that division is the operational inverse of multiplication. Thus, to divide 48 by 8, students should be instructed to first align 8 on the inside scale under 48 on the outside scale, then to find 1 on the inside scale and read the answer directly opposite it on the outside scale (in this case, 6). Again, repeated opportunities for practice should be provided.

Activities with the circular slide rule can also be extended to calculation with multidigit numbers. The procedure always remains the same (i.e., steps 1–4), but the slide rule can be used to approximate products through 1,000. For example, the same placement of the rule as explained above could be used to illustrate 60 × 8 = 480. The user must place the decimal point.

It should be noted, however, that the precise answer is not always forthcoming when multiplying larger numbers because of the inaccuracy in this particular slide rule and the adjustments that the student must make. Still, use of this rule forces children to estimate answers and to consider the reasonableness of their conclusions.

Evaluation: correct answers given to multiplication and division problems with the aid of the circular slide rule

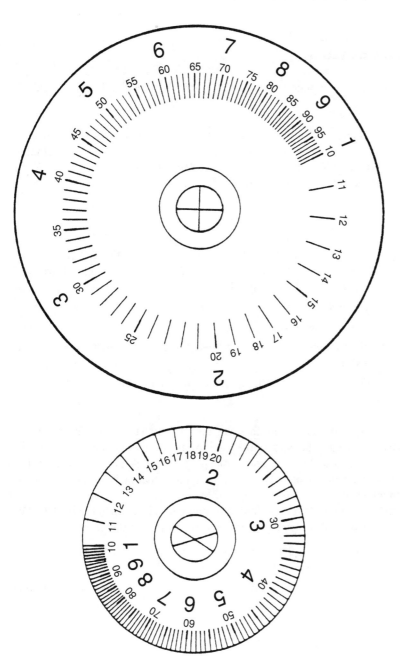

FIGURE 3.32
Circular slide-rule components

ACTIVITY TWELVE:

How Many Basic Facts Must One Learn?

Objective: to complete multiplication computations using either or both of the two finger methods

Materials: none needed

Procedure: The prospect of memorizing 100 multiplication facts is overwhelming for some students. Fortunately, by applying one or two mathematical principles and number tricks, that number can be reduced considerably. There really are not 100 distinct basic facts to learn. Refer to a multiplication chart and consider these points:

TOTAL
NUMBER
LEFT

$$100$$
$$\underline{-45} \quad (1)$$
$$55$$

$$\underline{-9} \quad (2)$$
$$45$$

$$\underline{-8} \quad (3)$$
$$36$$

$$\underline{-7} \quad (4)$$
$$31$$

1. Application of the commutative property of multiplication reduces the number from 100 to 55. This principle states that for all real numbers, $a \times b = b \times a$. It is thus necessary for the child to learn only about half of the total number of facts.

2. The zeros are easy.

3. The ones are easy.

4. The twos are also easy—children don't multiply by two, but double instead.

5. There are now 31 left, and ten of these are doubles (e.g., 5×5 and 8×8).

Children will need to spend some time practicing the remaining rules. Here are two number tricks that may help to ease the burden. Both are forms of finger multiplication. Please note that such "tricks" as these do not promote true understanding and therefore are not to be confused with basic developmental activities. It is assumed that such work has preceded the use of these methods.

The first method uses fingers to represent specific numbers, as shown in Figure 3.33. For the multiplication of two numbers, give your students the following directions.

1. Touch together the two fingers that represent the numbers you wish to multiply. For example, to multiply 8×7 the hands should be positioned as in Figure 3.34.

2. Count the number of fingers touching and below. This is the number of tens (in this problem, 5 tens or 50).

FIGURE 3.33
Number representation in the finger method

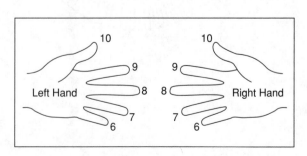

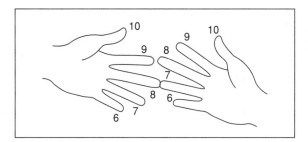

FIGURE 3.34
Finger method: 8 × 7

3. Multiply the number of fingers (including thumbs) above those touching on the left hand by those above the touching fingers on the right hand (here, 2 × 3 = 6).

4. To find the product, add the results of steps 2 and 3 (50 + 6 = 56; therefore, 8 × 7 = 56).

Students should be given more opportunities to calculate in this way until they can do this process quickly.

The second method is based on residuals over five. Using the same example of 8 × 7, students should be instructed to do the following:

1. Raise three fingers on the left hand (5 + 3 = 8) and two on the right hand (5 + 2 = 7). The total of the raised fingers is thus 5, representing the number of tens.

2. The number of fingers not raised on the left hand is 2, and on the right hand is 3. These represent the ones.

3. The product of these "down" fingers is six (2 × 3). This is added to the 50 generated above. The product of 8 and 7 is therefore 50 + 6 or 56.

Evaluation: correct answers to multiplication or division problems through use of either or both of the methods taught

ACTIVITY THIRTEEN:

Contig

Objective: to apply basic arithmetic facts in a game situation

Materials: Contig game board (Figure 3.35)

3 dice, rules

playing chips

Procedure: Contig is a math facts game that can be used by two or more players. It is suggested that you make a printed copy of the rules available to players along with the game board. This is a good game for your students to play independently when work is finished. The rules of the game are as follows.

The first player shakes the three dice. That player may add, subtract, multiply, or divide using each die only once. A chip is placed on the resulting number. Each player, in turn, repeats this procedure. The objective is to generate, using three dice, a number that appears next to a number that is already covered by a chip. A player earns one point for each chip the new number is touching. The person with the highest number of points wins the game.

Evaluation: participation in the game by each student

FIGURE 3.35
Contig game board

1	2	3	4	5	6	7	8
9	10	11	12	13	14	15	16
17	18	19	20	21	22	23	24
25	26	27	28	29	30	31	32
33	34	35	36	37	38	39	40
41	42	44	45	48	50	54	55
60	64	66	72	75	80	90	96
100	108	120	125	144	150	180	216

ACTIVITY FOURTEEN:

Krypto

Objective: to correctly use computation skills to play the Krypto game

Materials: 52 cards, marked as directed

Procedure: Krypto is played with a deck of 52 cards, numbered from 1 to 25. There are

> 3 cards each of the numbers from 1 to 10
>
> 2 cards each of the numbers from 11 to 17
>
> 1 card each of the numbers from 18 to 25

The object of the game is to combine five cards (the hand) to equal the sixth card (the objective, or Krypto card) by using only the rules of simple arithmetic. Two to eight students can play. The rules of the game are as follows.

Each player draws a card from the deck. The player with the highest card deals first. Thereafter, the winner of each hand is the next dealer. Five cards are dealt to each player, numbered side down. The cards remain down until the dealer turns up the Krypto card (the next card in the deck). As this is done, all players pick up their hands and begin to play. The aim of each player is to use the numbers on each card in his or her hand to equal the Krypto card by using addition, subtraction, multiplication, or division. *Each card must be used once and only once.* The first player to use all five cards to match the Krypto card says "Krypto" and verifies how his or her cards were combined to get that number. One point is scored for each correct solution. A new hand is then dealt and the play continues.

1. Cut a sheet of construction paper in half the long way. Have students fold each part into four sections and tape the two parts together.

2. Have students make frame of tagboard.

3.

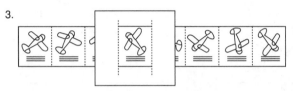

FIGURE 3.36
Frame book

Evaluation: participation in Krypto games, ability to perform correctly the computations required in the game

UNIT EVALUATION: FRAME BOOK

Have each student follow the instructions in Figure 3.36 to make an individual frame book that explains a favorite mnemonic. Each page should have at least one sentence and a visual. Frame books can be used for any unit evaluation.

ADDITIONAL ACTIVITIES:

Extension and Evaluation

1. Have students devise additional mnemonic devices.

2. Students can survey others to see whether they know or use any mnemonics. Discuss the findings in class.

3. Have students keep a daily journal about mnemonics and how they used them throughout the unit.

4. Have students examine books such as *Codes* by Nigel Nelson, Thomson Learning, 1994.

5. Use activities from a source such as *Memory Development* by Luther Misenheimer, Costa Mesa, CA: Saddleback Educational Inc., 1991.

6. Check the Internet for other examples of mnemonics used in classrooms around the world.

Teacher Resources

Brain Teasers! Over 180 Quick Activities & Worksheets That Make Kids Think. Culver City, CA: Social Studies School Services, 1994. (K–6)

See Appendix B for additional resources and addresses.

PATTERNS

Patterns: Prediction of regularity and patterns through experimentation and systematic data collection permit the student to deduce several fundamental principles of the physical sciences.

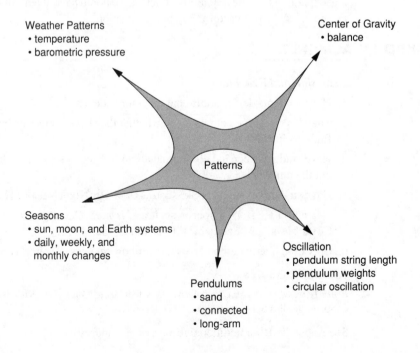

Weather Patterns
• temperature
• barometric pressure

Center of Gravity
• balance

Patterns

Seasons
• sun, moon, and Earth systems
• daily, weekly, and
  monthly changes

Oscillation
• pendulum string length
• pendulum weights
• circular oscillation

Pendulums
• sand
• connected
• long-arm

INTRODUCTION

All of the systems we observe display changes. Many systems change from a first state to a second state and then back to the first. A pendulum is a classic example of a system that displays regular oscillations. A few other systems that children know of or can easily understand include the following:

1. *The sun-moon-Earth system.* The sun's apparent position changes, but the change repeats itself every 24 hours. The moon's position changes but it goes through one change from full moon to new to full every $29\frac{1}{2}$ days and exhibits 13 of these phases per year.

2. *The climate of a region.* Climate changes during the seasons but repeats itself every year. Short-range weather patterns are very complex, but variations from sunny periods to cloudy periods often show a cycle of about 7 days.

3. *The rise and fall of rivers.* Rivers respond to a variety of climatic conditions. Seasonal melting of snow and monsoon rains are but two of the causes.

4. *The growth of plants.* Growth is a function of climate, and most plants in temperate zones emerge in the spring, flourish during the summer, and go into a resting or dormant stage during dry and cold periods.

In this unit, you should introduce the concept of systems that change in a predictable way. You may wish to show how a pendulum swings and retraces the same path over and over. Through discussion about the motion of the sun, the polar angle of Earth, the path of Earth, and the resulting seasonal phenomena, expand the children's awareness of the many oscillating systems that exist. Describe how seasons are related to a host of naturally recurring changes, such as the rising and falling of rivers, plant growth cycles, and seasonal bird migrations.

You will also want to point out that an oscillating system often will "force" oscillation in a new system. As an example, explain that the vibrating strings of a guitar force the sounding box to vibrate, generating audible sound waves in the air. There are also systems that resonate with each other. Just as a pendulum has a particular period, so does the back-and-forth motion of the springs of a car. Almost everyone has at one time or another driven over a dirt road with washboards. The washboards or arrangement of piles of dirt across the road are generated by many cars. Each car's springs are resonant with the others. Each oscillating set of springs builds the washboards, which in turn set the next car's springs into rhythmical oscillations.

As in other units, you can use a film or book about seasons, pendulums, weather, or even bird migration to introduce the unit theme and begin to expand the children's understanding of cycles and oscillations. After reviewing and discussing the book or film, you may wish to develop a web, starting, if you like, with the web presented at the beginning of this unit.

Following that introduction, you may begin to use some or all of the eight activities that follow. The first six of these activities deal with several kinds and arrangements of pendulums. Throughout these activities, be sure to give your students ample time to play with the different pendulums they construct, as well as a large space like a gym or open stairwell to work in. The remaining two activities relate to balance and weather patterns.

All of these activities can be used as guides and need not be followed in any particular order. After some basic understandings have been developed, encourage groups of children to go beyond the suggestions and explore other systems that change from one state to another in a regular, predictable way. In particular, you may want to work with those systems with which children are most familiar, such as the seasons of the year. No matter what or how many patterns and systems you investigate, your students are sure to benefit from their new understandings of the order that exists in the world around them.

Unit Objectives. Students will:

1. learn about some common systems, such as the seasons of the year and the sun-moon-Earth system, and how they bring about changes.
2. learn about different kinds and characteristics of pendulums.
3. build an understanding of the effects of systems on their lives and the lives of others around them.

Appropriate Grade Levels. Elementary and Middle School

Vocabulary.

systems	oscillation
pendulum	cycles

Note: See Appendix A for planning sheets.

ACTIVITY ONE:

Making a Simple Pendulum

Objective: to make and use a simple pendulum, and to explore how to change its period

Materials: small pieces of cardboard

string

masking tape

weights (e.g., washers, fishing sinkers, nuts, or bolts)

Procedure: Give your students the following directions, either orally or in writing.

1. Take a piece of string and push it through the hole in your piece of cardboard. Tie a knot, and then fasten the cardboard to the underside of your desk with masking tape. In this way, your desk is supporting your pendulum. Now tie a weight to the loose end of your string.

2. You may instead fasten a stick between two desks and fasten the string to the stick if you prefer. This may give your pendulum more room in which to swing, and you could share it with a friend.

Be sure to allow sufficient time for students to assemble and mount their pendulums, repeating directions or giving assistance as needed.

Once the pendulums are ready, explain to students that the period of a pendulum is the time duration for a complete back-and-forth swing or oscillation. Allow students a minute or two to set their pendulums in motion and to time their periods. Then explain that they are to try to find out how they can change the period of the pendulum. To get them started, tell them that one way they might change the period is to start the swing in different places.

Next, ask students to try to think of three changes they could make with their pendulums that might change the period, and write those possibilities down. Then divide the class into several small groups in which students will share their ideas with each other. You may want to appoint a recorder to write down some of the suggestions of the group members. Finally, have students test each of the suggestions. When they are finished, they should circle those suggestions that did change the period of the pendulum. End with a discussion time during which the findings of each group are shared.

Evaluation: completion of pendulum and ability to name ways in which a pendulum's period can be changed

ACTIVITY TWO:

Pendulum String Lengths and Oscillations

Objective: to measure and graph the relationship between changes in the arm lengths of pendulums and their periods of oscillation

Materials: string

weights

tape

cardboard

Pendulum Chart and Graph (Figure 3.37) for each student

Procedure: Review the findings of Activity One by pointing out that the students probably found out that the length of the string is related to the pendulum's oscillation period. Tell them that, while they have no way of testing it, a change in the pull of gravity would change the period. The period would, in fact, get longer as the pull of gravity decreased. Ask students whether they think that a pendulum would work in a spaceship or space laboratory, or on the moon.

FIGURE 3.37
Pendulum chart and graph forms

Length of arm in cm	Number of seconds per 10 swings

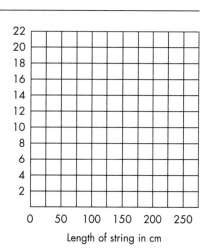

Ask for volunteers to complete this sentence: The longer the string, the _____ the period of the pendulum. Then tell your class that their next investigation will be to find out whether a pendulum with a 21-cm string, making 10 oscillations in 10 seconds, will make 10 oscillations in 20 seconds if it is changed so that the string is 42-cm long.

Before they begin, explain to students that all relationships are not linear. That is, when one variable (such as pendulum length) changes, the other variable (period) changes, too, but if you plot length versus period, the points on the grid do not lie in a straight line. After eliciting some guesses as to the kind of pattern or curve several such points (length of pendulum arm vs. period) would make, have students carry out the experiment. While doing so, have them collect data and plot them on the Pendulum Chart and Graph Forms shown in Figure 3.37. Note that they will be making several variations of string length.

When students are finished, tell them to look carefully at their curves and predict the answer to the following questions:

1. If you make a pendulum with a 3-meter-long string, how many swings do you predict this pendulum would make in 10 seconds?

2. How long would the pendulum string have to be if the pendulum were to make 10 swings in one minute?

Evaluation: completion of pendulum experiment and the recordings of the results on the Pendulum Chart and Graph Forms

ACTIVITY THREE:

Pendulum Weights and Oscillations

Objective: to make paper-cup pendulums and to measure and record the effects of varying weights on the period of oscillation

Materials: Slinky spring, or several rubber bands tied together   paper clips

paper cups with sand in them   washers

Slinky Pendulum Chart and Graph Forms (Figure 3.39)

Procedure: If students have completed Activities One and Two, they have by now discovered that the period of a pendulum is related to the string, or arm, length. They are now going to determine how long the string should be so that their pendulums oscillate once in one second. They will again each need to use a short piece of stick, string, and a small weight to set up the pendulum under their desks. Because this pendulum must be an accurate minute-measuring device and will be used for several other activities, it should be made with care.

Once this timing pendulum has been completed by each student, you are ready to begin the next step of the experiment. To do so, you will need a Slinky spring or a chain of rubber bands, a cup, and some sand. If you don't have a Slinky, tie the rubber bands together instead. Then set up the oscillating Slinky or rubber-band pendulum as shown in Figure 3.38. Note that the paper cup is fastened to the Slinky or rubber bands with three bent paper clips.

Point out to students that the oscillation in this case consists of an up-and-down rather than a back-and-forth motion. Remind them that in Activity One, when they added weights to their pendulum, the addition did not seem to change the period. They should now place a few weights in the cup so that the Slinky is stretched to about 24 inches (about 61 cm). Someone

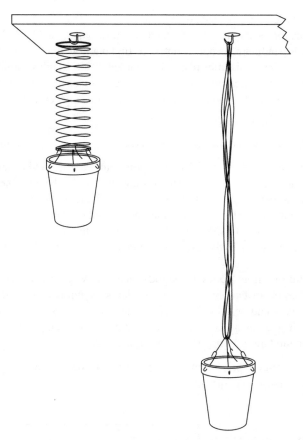

FIGURE 3.38
Slinky and rubber-band pendulums

FIGURE 3.39
Slinky pendulum chart and graph forms

Weight (number of same-sized washers in cup)	Number of oscillations in 10 seconds

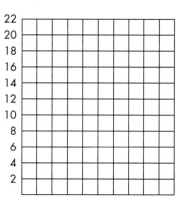

Weight or number of same-sized washers

Number of oscillations in 10 seconds

should then start it oscillating up and down, keeping in mind that now one oscillation or period is the time it takes for the cup to move to the down position, up, and back down again. Have students start their pendulum second-counters to find out how many times the Slinky oscillates in 10 seconds. Once this information is recorded, some weights should be removed or added, and the new period measured and recorded. Have students complete the following sentences, which could be written on the board while they are conducting their experiment:

1. When the cup was lighter, the spring oscillated _____ times in 10 seconds.
2. When the cup was heavier, the spring oscillated _____ times in 10 seconds.

If students are surprised by their findings, point out that this kind of an oscillating system *does* change its period as the bob weight is changed. Ask what else they think could be changed to alter the period of the Slinky system, and list all of the ideas expressed on the board. Have students then select one idea that interests them or their group and change their Slinky system accordingly to find out whether making this one change does change the period of their system. Remind them to use their pendulum second-timers and to check their results carefully.

Finally, ask this question: "Does the period of the Slinky system versus weight in the cup generate a set of points that are linear?" Have students, individually or within small groups, guess whether this would be a linear set of points or a nonlinear set of points. Have them follow up on their guesses by collecting data and checking their results, using the Slinky Pendulum Chart and Graph Forms shown in Figure 3.39.

Evaluation: completion of paper-cup pendulums, the experiments described using them, and the recorded results of those experiments

ACTIVITY FOUR:

Pendulum String Length and Number of Oscillations

Objective: to vary the string length of a pendulum and measure the corresponding changes in the number of oscillations

Materials: Tinkertoys

string pendulums, two per child

paper clips

Modified-pendulum Chart and Graph Forms (Figure 3.40)

Procedure: To carry out this experiment, each student will again need a minute-measuring pendulum. Each student will also need to make a simple Tinkertoy frame from which a single pendulum is suspended. Once all equipment is set up and ready to use, give students the following directions.

1. Swing your one-second timing pendulum and record the number of times it oscillates in 10 seconds.

2. Make a second pendulum but make the string 2 inches (about 5 cm) shorter and suspend it from the same frame. Swing only the first pendulum. Record what happens to the second one.

3. Now swing both at the same time. Which one stops first? Did anything else happen to the one that stopped? Record your results.

FIGURE 3.40
Modified-pendulum chart and graph forms

Amount shortened on 2nd pendulum	Number of swings 1st pendulum makes before stopping

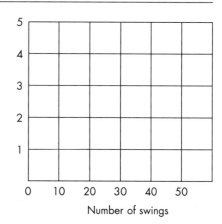

Amount of shortened interval (in inches)

Number of swings

4. Change the strings so that both pendulums supported from the frame are the same length. Now swing them together, and record what happens.

   Tell your students that this strange effect can be seen even more clearly if two very long pendulums are suspended from a string stretched across the top of a doorway or between two light fixtures. The two pendulum strings should be fastened, about a foot apart from each other, to the cross-string. (You will probably want to do this activity with the whole class at once because of space requirements.) Once this is set up, one student should start one pendulum swinging while the others count the number of oscillations it makes before stopping completely. Then, have a student shorten the string so that it is one inch shorter. The modified pendulum should be swung again and the number of oscillations again counted and recorded. The string should continuously be shortened in one-inch intervals, with the counting and recording repeated each time on the Modified-Pendulum Chart and Graph Forms shown in Figure 3.40.

   Complete the activity by having the class discuss how the second pendulum could be changed so that the first would stop when its bob makes 40 oscillations. Finish by having students check their ideas for accuracy.

Evaluation: completion of the experiments described and the recording of the results of those experiments

ACTIVITY FIVE:

Oscillations of Coupled Pendulums

Objective: to observe the effects of a coupling rod on the oscillations of two pendulums

Materials:
10 rubber bands

2 thumbtacks

a light stick about 15 inches long

2 paper cups about half-full of sand

6 paper clips

2 white paper "targets"

paper and pencils

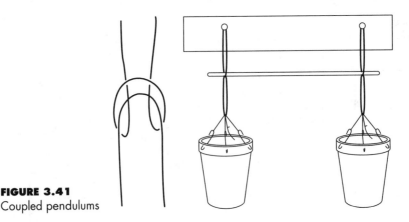

FIGURE 3.41
Coupled pendulums

Procedure: For this activity, students will need to make two chains of rubber bands, fastened together as shown in Figure 3.41, and attach them to the underside of a desk with thumbtacks. The stick, which will serve as a coupling rod, can be slid between any of the rubber-band loops and moved from one to another as desired. Each cup should be fastened to the lower end of a rubber-band chain using bent paper clips. When it is complete, the apparatus should look like the illustration shown in Figure 3.41.

When everything is ready to use, instruct students to remove the coupling rod and pull down on one cup, starting it oscillating. They should then observe whether or not the second cup begins to oscillate. Next, they should insert the coupling rod and repeat the procedure, observing what happens. Bring out, through discussion if possible, that the force needed to start the motionless pendulum comes from the one that is moving, with the force carried from one pendulum to the other through the coupling.

Now ask students to consider why one pendulum stops completely and then starts again. Why doesn't the system come to a balance (with both pendulums oscillating uniformly) and just keep going? The final part of the activity involves fastening two white paper "targets" to the ends of the coupling rod. These targets will help students focus on the motion of the coupling rod. They should try various combinations of weights in the cups and various placements of the rod in the rubber-band loops. As always in experiments, they should keep a record of what happens as the system is changed.

Finish with a class discussion in which the following questions are considered.

1. What things determine whether the targets move up and down together, or whether one moves up and the other moves down?

2. What determines the time duration from when both ends of the coupling rod are moving up and down together until, after moving in opposite directions, they again move together?

Evaluation: completion of the outlined experiments, participation in class discussions

ACTIVITY SIX:

Circular Oscillations

Objective: to observe and record the movements of circular oscillations of a pendulum

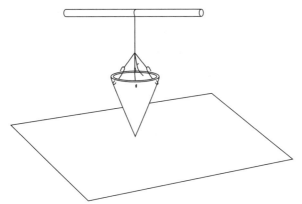

FIGURE 3.42
Pendulum with circular oscillation

Materials: pendulum support (a board laid across a table will work)

sifted sand or table salt

a paper cone

string

Procedure: Begin the activity by reminding the class that the pendulums made up to this point have oscillated back and forth or up and down. In working with these pendulums, they have found something out about the factors that determine the oscillation period. In contrast, the pendulum that they will now make, which also will be suspended from a string, can be swung in a circular pattern.

Help your students set the equipment up as illustrated in Figure 3.42, and then fill the cone with the sand or salt. Lay a large sheet of brown paper under where the cone is hanging. When you are ready to begin, cut a hole in the bottom of the cone and swing it in a circle. It won't always follow a circle, but try!

If you wish to keep a record of the patterns, use salt on black paper and photograph it from above, or trace the pattern with pencils of different colors. Ask students to look and see how well you did at swinging the cone in a perfect circle. Point out that, as the salt or sand came from the cone, the ridge that built up was thicker in some places than others. Ask whether anyone can explain this. Ask students to come up with a rule for it by filling in the blanks in these sentences:

1. The faster the cone travels, the _____ salt there is in the ridge.
2. The slower the cone travels, the _____ salt there is in the ridge.

Then ask students to look carefully at the patterns. Ask them to find the part of the patterns that has thin ridges and the part that has thick ridges. At this point, you may want to repeat the procedure several times, involving students directly in the experiment and comparing the results. After several patterns have been made and recorded, draw on the board three pictures of patterns that the cone might make. They should look something like those shown in Figure 3.43. Ask students to mark an *X* where they think the ridge would be the thickest and an *O* where they think the cone was travelling the fastest.

Evaluation: completion of described experiment, participation in group discussions

FIGURE 3.43
Circular oscillation patterns

ACTIVITY SEVEN:

Finding the Center of Gravity

Objective: to balance objects or shapes by finding their centers of gravity

Materials: construction paper cut-outs   a bottle

string   two forks

two corks   two straight pins

Procedure: Ask students whether any of them have ever watched a circus high-wire or tightrope walker. Bring out in your discussion that most performers use an umbrella or a long pole to help them keep their balance. Discuss why this might be so.

Then discuss how an object on a string could be balanced. Instruct each student to cut out objects from construction paper. Suggest symmetrical shapes, such as butterflies or leaves, or circus items or performers. Stretch several strings across the room so that everyone will have room in which to work. Students should then try to get their shapes to balance on the string. An ongoing discussion of students' experiences and discoveries should be helpful.

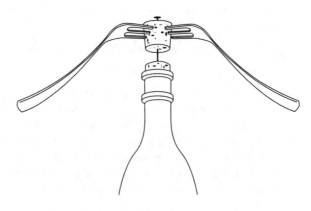

FIGURE 3.44
Balancing activity

Whether or not students have difficulty, you may wish to carry out the following activity, which is illustrated in Figure 3.44. Take two corks, a bottle, two forks, and two pins. Push one cork into the opening of the bottle and stick one of the pins into the center of the cork. Stick the remaining pin into the unused cork. Then see whether anyone can get the other cork and the two forks to balance on the pin in the bottle. Discuss successes and failures and try to conclude by coming up with an explanation of how and why objects in both activities balanced as they did.

Evaluation: completion of balancing activities, participation in class discussions

ACTIVITY EIGHT:

Discovering Weather Patterns

Objective: to record and examine temperature and barometric pressure patterns for various U.S. locations

Materials: daily newspapers

paper and pencils (graph paper, although not essential, is advisable)

Procedure: With your class, select several locations in the United States. Using the daily paper, look up and record the temperature and barometric pressure, if it is available, at these locations. After about 2 weeks, plot the temperatures and pressures on a graph. In most cases, a rhythmic change pattern will show up. Ask students whether it is possible to predict weather from the graph.

You might wish to first conduct, or at least begin, this activity with the class as a whole. Once students understand the procedures of the activity, have students each choose a city of their own on which to focus. Individual students will then look up and record daily temperatures and plot the points on a graph. Guide students' selections so that your class is considering weather in all parts of the country.

Then you might want to look at the larger picture of weather. Most weather bureaus keep yearly records of weather that are available in publications describing seasonal weather changes. Ask your school librarian to secure such a record. From this, help your students develop graphs showing yearly fluctuations in temperature, sunshine, precipitation, and air pressure. Point out to them that such information is important in making estimates of heating costs, needed fuel supplies, and even water costs for keeping a lawn green during the summer. In light of recent energy developments, ask students why designers of solar-heated houses need this kind of information.

Evaluation: completion of group and/or individual weather graphs

UNIT EVALUATION: CLASS VIDEO

Have students work in small groups to plan segments of a video to summarize the learning that has taken place in this unit. A class video could be applied to any unit.

ADDITIONAL ACTIVITIES:

Extension and Evaluation

1. If you can locate one, bring in a croquet (pendulum) game for your students to enjoy. Or, make one of your own, building a wooden frame containing six parallel rungs from which an equal number of string-attached balls are suspended. Have students note the effects of one swinging ball upon the others.

2. Have students set up a display of various types of pendulums, games that use pendulums, books about pendulums, and so on. Invite another class to view the display and have teams of students explain or demonstrate the various parts of the display.

3. Make a collection of books about seasons for students to pursue additional reading.

4. Use the Internet for students to investigate seasons in other parts of the United States or the world.

Teacher Resources

See Appendix B for additional resources and addresses.

Epilogue

Singer Peggy Lee a few years back recorded a song entitled "Is That All There Is?" You might very well be asking that question at this point. Is that all there is to an integrated approach? The answer is an emphatic yes and no! Yes, because conceptually this approach is fairly simplistic, it does make sense, and it can be ably defended from a number of perspectives. We have attempted to do just that in this book. No, because there are literally an infinite number of permutations that this approach can take, and one can never really master all of the whats, whys, and wherefores. There will always be that simple investigation that could have been carried out and for one reason or another never was, or those general directions not pursued that might have improved the overall quality of the theme.

Teaching involves a great deal of judgment. Good teachers make good judgments more often than they make bad ones. As you become more comfortable with this approach you will undoubtedly begin to routinely make better judgments. This will be an exciting time for you intellectually, one that will be forever changing and one that will be as much (or more) of a challenge for you as it is for the children. It is a great opportunity to build on all you have learned in your methods courses and an excellent time to work with a team of other interested teachers in your school.

As a parting thought, we would like to suggest some teacher behaviors that have proven effective in the past and that are worth remembering as you embark on this new teaching and learning adventure.

1. Introduce the theme in a flexible manner that not only allows the children to relate it to their particular situation, but also opens up various avenues of potential investigation.

2. Serve as a coordinator and collaborator. Assist, rather than direct, individuals or groups of students as they investigate different aspects of the problem.

3. Involve students regularly in project or theme activities. This regularity will allow the children to have a chance to become involved in the challenge and carry out comprehensive investigations.

4. Provide the tools and supplies necessary for initial hands-on work in the classroom. Later on, children can become partially responsible for the location, procurement, and development of needed materials.

5. Be patient. Allow the children to make their own mistakes and to find their own way. But do offer assistance and point out sources of help if the children become frustrated in their approach to the problem.

6. Provide frequent opportunities for group reports and student exchanges of ideas in class discussions. In most cases, based on their own critical examination of the procedures they have used, students will improve or set new directions in their investigations.

7. Ask higher-level questions (questions not answerable with a single word or fact) to stimulate thinking.

8. Make sure that groups are appropriately constituted and that the criteria for group involvement are continually varied. This will ensure the broadest possible set of experiences for each individual.

9. Remember that success is defined differently. It is not simply the mastery of specific bits of knowledge, although this is sure to occur. It is not only the following of a particular line of investigation predetermined by the teacher. Success in an integrated study is defined by the progress that students make toward the solution of a particular problem or concern. Success is defined in terms of process as much as it is defined in terms of specific product outcomes. Evaluate accordingly!

Planning Forms

I. WEBBING DIAGRAM

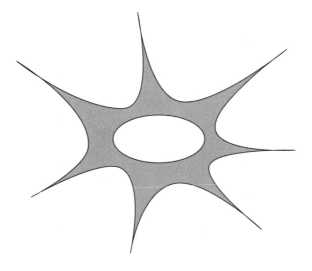

II. KWL SHEET

What We **K**now	What We **W**ant to Know	What We **L**earned

III. UNIT OBJECTIVES CHART

OBJECTIVES
Students will:

	Lesson Number								
	1	2	3	4	5	6	7	8	*
1. _____ _____ _____									
2. _____ _____ _____									
3. _____ _____ _____									
4. _____ _____ _____									
5. _____ _____ _____									
6. _____ _____ _____									
7. _____ _____ _____									
8. _____ _____ _____									
9. _____ _____									

IV. VOCABULARY CHART

VOCABULARY						Lesson Number						
	1	2	3	4	5	6	7	8	9	10	*	
• _____												
• _____												
• _____												
• _____												
• _____												
• _____												
• _____												
• _____												
• _____												
• _____												
• _____												
• _____												
• _____												
• _____												
• _____												
• _____												
• _____												

V. INDIVIDUAL ACTIVITY PLAN

ACTIVITY _____ : _____

Objective:

Materials:

Procedure:

Evaluation:

VI. CURRICULUM AREAS CHART

CURRICULUM AREAS	1	2	3	4	5	Activity Number 6	7	8	9	10	*
Whole Language											
Mathematics											
Science											
Social Studies											
Physical Education											
Arts											
Music											

VII. LEARNING STYLES CHART

LEARNING STYLES	1	2	3	4	5	Activity Number 6	7	8	9	10	*
Linguistic											
Logical/Mathematical											
Visual											
Musical											
Kinesthetic											
Intrapersonal											
Interpersonal											

VIII. LEVELS OF QUESTIONS CHART

LEVELS OF QUESTIONS	Activity Number										
	1	2	3	4	5	6	7	8	9	10	*
Knowledge											
Comprehension											
Application											
Analysis											
Synthesis											
Evaluation											

IX. INCLUSION CHART

INCLUSION	Activity Number										
	1	2	3	4	5	6	7	8	9	10	*
Multicultural											
Gender-fair											
Disabled											

X. INCLUSION CHECKLIST

_____ Do I accept each child as he or she is?

_____ Do I help all children feel they belong?

_____ Do I show confidence in my students?

_____ Do I let them know I like them?

_____ Do I make each child feel that he or she has something to contribute?

_____ Do I help them accept one another?

_____ Do I let everyone express his or her feelings?

_____ Do I live up to agreements with students?

_____ Do I succeed in getting everyone to assume some responsibility?

_____ Do I help the group form a behavior code?

XI. UNIT OBJECTIVES CHECKLIST

Names	Objectives						Evaluation		
	1	2	3	4	5	6	Test	KWL	Group Project

XII. GROUP EVALUATION SHEET

OUR GROUP _____

1. We shared ideas.

   _____
   YES   SOME   NO

2. We all participated.

   _____
   YES   SOME   NO

3. We stayed on-task.

   _____
   YES   SOME   NO

4. We used our time wisely.

   _____
   YES   SOME   NO

5. We praised others.

   _____
   YES   SOME   NO

Signed _____

_____

_____

XIII. SELF-EVALUATION SHEET

Name _____ Unit _____

Date _____

I learned _____.

I made _____.

I read _____.

I wrote _____.

I shared _____.

I cooperated _____.

I liked _____.

XIV. SAMPLE LETTER HOME

From _____   Date _____

Today we began a unit with _____ as our theme. I hope you will discuss with your child what we are doing at school. The following might be questions you could ask your child:

What do you think _____?

What are three _____?

Have you read a special book about _____?

What have you made _____?

We are creating a _____ display. We would appreciate any items you could share with us. We especially need _____. Please label your items so we can easily return them.

If you would be able to share any personal experiences with the class or share any items with the class, please let me know by returning the form below.

Thanks.

_____

I could:

_____ go on a field trip.

_____ share _____.

_____ loan you _____.

Signed _____

Date _____

General Resources

TEACHER RESOURCES

Perma-Bound Books
Vandalia Road
Jacksonville, IL 62650
1-800-637-6581
(lists books by thematic units)

Jackdaw Publications
PO Box 503
Amawalk, NY 10501
1-800-789-0022
(portfolios of historical documents)

Carson-Dellosa Publishing, Inc.
PO Box 35665
Greensboro, NC 27425
1-800-321-0943
(thematic units)

Milbrook Press, Inc.
2 Old New Milford Road
Box 335
Brookfield, CT 06804
1-800-462-4703
(thematic series)

Saddleback Educational, Inc.
3505 Cadillac Ave.
Building F-9
Costa Mesa, CA 92626
1-714-540-4010
(thematic units)

Social Studies School Service (SSSS)
10200 Jefferson Blvd., Room P
PO Box 802
Culver City, CA 90232-0802
1-800-421-4246
(resources for Grade K-6)

Children's Press/Franklin Watts/Orchard Books
Curriculum Division
5440 North Cumberland Ave.
Chicago, IL 60656-1494
1-800-621-1115
(books for children)

Thomson Learning
115 Fifth Ave.
New York, NY 10003
1-800-880-4253
(books for children)

Troll Books
100 Corporate Drive
Mahwah, NJ 07430
1-800-526-6289 (ext. 1118)
(books for children)

Greenhaven Press, Inc.
PO Box 289009
San Diego, CA 92198
1-800-231-5163
(Opposing Viewpoints Junior Series)

Good Apple/Fearon Teacher Aids/Modern
Curriculum Press and Judy/Instructo
4350 Equity Drive
PO Box 2649
Columbus, OH 43216
1-800-321-3106
(thematic units)

Teacher-Created Materials
PO Box 1040
Huntington Beach, CA 92647
1-800-662-4321
(thematic units)

Instructional Fair, Inc.
Grand Rapids, MI

Activity Resources Co.
PO Box 4875
Hayward, CA 94540
1-510-782-1300

**National Council of Teachers
of Mathematics (NCTM)**
P.O. Box 25405
Richmond, VA 23260-5405
Telephone   (703) 620-9840
Fax   (703) 476-2970
(Ask for Educational Materials Catalog.)

Sunburst Communications
101 Castleton Street
PO Box 100
Pleasantville, NY 10570
1-800-321-7511
(educational software)

The Internet
(Of course, the Internet is fast becoming *the* premier
resource for information generally and
interdisciplinary topics specifically. We encourage
all users of this book to become involved in the
Internet—the rewards will be great.

INDEX

For more information on Merrill Education products
visit our Internet home page at
http://www.smartpages.com/merrill

ISBN 0-13-227778-6

9 780132 277785